Thinking Outside the Bulb

The Art of Creating an Amazing Customer Experience

Mike Dandridge

Copyright© 2004
By Michael E. Dandridge
All Rights Reserved.
Printed in the United States of America

All Scripture citation is from the HOLY BIBLE, NEW INTERNATIONAL VERSION® by Zondervan Publishing.

ISBN: 1-59196-423-7
1. Business development 2. Customer Service

High Voltage Productions
Dallas, Texas

To Mark Adair

who taught me, "it's okay to have fun at work."

I DON'T KNOW WHAT YOUR DESTINY WILL BE, BUT ONE THING I DO KNOW: THE ONLY ONES AMONG YOU WHO WILL BE REALLY HAPPY ARE THOSE WHO HAVE SOUGHT AND FOUND — *HOW TO SERVE.*

ALBERT SCHWEITZER

TABLE OF CONTENTS

THE HEART OF YOUR CUSTOMER – PAGE VI
BACK TO THE BASICS – PAGE VIII

INNOVATION - 1
1. It's Showtime! - 3
2. Look Mom, No Hands! - 9
3. Value is in the Eyes of the Customer - 13
4. Competing With a Mouse - 19
5. Make it Easy - 21
6. Know Thy Customer - 25
7. Just Say Yes! - 29

COMMITMENT - 33
8. Turning Customers Into Prospects - 35
9. Just a Note to Say Thanks - 39
10. How to Deal With Difficult Customers - 43
11. The Magic of 30 - 47
12. When Bad Things Happen to Good Customers - 51
13. Follow Up - 55
14. "Plays Well With Others" - 57

KNOWLEDGE - 61
15. That's What I'm Talking About - 63
16. Read Your Customer's Magazines - 67
17. The 2% Solution - 69
18. Save the World and Be in Bed by 10 - 73
19. I know you think you heard what I said… - 77
20. Think Outside the Bulb - 79
21. If You Could Read Their Minds - 81
22. Ignorance is No Excuse - 85

INTEGRITY - 89
23. Would You Buy From You? - 91
24. Why Would I Buy From You? - 93
25. Act Enthusiastic and You'll Be Enthusiastic - 95
26. Let Me Be Honest With You - 99
27. Watch Your Mouth - 101

INITIATIVE - 105
   28. Did I Ask You? - 107
   29. Service That Delights - 111
   30. Do You Want to Be Right or Rich? - 115
   31. The Extra One - 117
   32. Does Everyone Know Who You Work For? - 119
   33. Do You Know Who You Work For? - 121
   34. What Customer Service Can't Do - 123

PROFESSIONALISM - 127
   35. Your One-Size-Fits-All Doesn't - 129
   36. For Faster Service Press "1" - 133
   37. You've Got Mail! - 137
   38. Be a Quick Change Artist - 139
   39. Blame it On the Microwave - 143
   40. First Impressions Last - 147
   41. Casual Friday is Out - 149

OWNERSHIP - 153
   42. We May Doze, But We Never Close - 155
   43. Shut Up and Have a Nice Day - 157
   44. Lighten Up! - 159
   45. See Yourself Succeeding - 161
   46. Mr. Potato Head, Unplugged - 163
   47. Are Your Customers Invisible? - 165
   48. A Satisfied Customer Never Is – 167
   49. Do You Speaka My Language? - 169
   50. Want Fries With That? - 171
   51. The Most Important One – 175
   Final Thought – 177
About the Author – 181

Special Thanks…

…to Bobby Casilhas, David Gifford, Tommy Grisham, Pam Hensley, Mark Hessing, Joe Holton, Mike Marlin, Bruce Scott, Steven Scott, and Drew Simpson. Your dedication, loyalty and friendship means more to me than you can ever know.

And deepest thanks to my wife, Frances; your servant's heart continues to teach me the value and satisfaction in serving others. Whatever measure of success I've enjoyed is a direct result of your love, encouragement and prayers.

The Heart of Your Customer

Customer expectations are at an all time high. Unfortunately, Customer Service is at an all time low.

S**URVEY SAYS – Mediocre to atrocious!**

When Gallup asked consumers to grade Customer Service for major businesses, including airlines, banks, supermarkets, restaurants, hotels and hospitals, the ratings were consistent – consistent in a negative way. "Mediocre to atrocious," was the box most often checked.

And as Customer Service continues to decline, customers' expectations are becoming even more demanding.

Mass production evolved into mass personalization. Technology makes it possible to customize each production unit through a simple series of keystrokes. Now customers really can have it their way.

Meanwhile, the emphasis on Customer Service shifted as the warehouse shopping experience caught on and service personnel became harder to find. The philosophy behind the new wave of mega-discount stores seemed to be *price everything cheap and let the customer fend for herself.*

LOOKING FOR BOBW

But, as Customers, we want the Best of Both Worlds. We enjoy the benefits of the new economy – competitive pricing, quality product, fast delivery – but we long for the traditions of the old. We miss the human connection and community. We still want "service with a smile." Technology changes, but our hearts remain the same.

This book is about blending the best of the new economy – innovation, knowledge, and initiative – with the principles of the old – professionalism, ownership, integrity and commitment. It's about building a business that is vibrant, passionate and focused on what customers want.

And a business like that can thrive in any economy.

BACK TO THE BASICS

Maybe it's time we got back to the basics…Chips Moman

This book is the outcome of thirty years of solid business experience. In writing it, there is one thing I take for granted – that you have a quality product or service that people want. If you don't have that, none of what you are about to read will help.

In other words, if you sell a product of inferior quality, it doesn't matter how wonderful your service is, people still won't buy it. If you own a restaurant where the food is lousy, no amount of bright, cheery servers will draw in customers. If the guests' bathrooms are dirty in your luxury hotel, free cookies and milk at bedtime won't bring you returning patrons.

First, get the basics right.

The 7 Phases of Amazing Customer Service

Amazing Customer Service doesn't begin and end at your place of business. It doesn't punch a clock, leave for lunch, or take a break. Amazing Customer Service is a frame of mind, an attitude that becomes who you are: a person who helps others. And the better you become at serving others, the more you will find that the world serves you in return.

Professionalism

Communicate a consistent, solid image that matches your customer's perception of professionalism for your industry. Presenting a professional image creates a doorway to success and prosperity.

Ownership
Customers love the person who can own up to a problem, a mistake or a challenge and turn it into a triumph. Being accountable to your customers sets you apart from your competitors.

Innovation
"New and improved" is a tired and meaningless cliché. True innovation sheds new light on familiar challenges. Customers are looking for the "next big thing." By bringing constant innovation to your organization, you will stay fresh and relevant in today's rapidly changing business landscape.

Knowledge
It's amazing how often we hear the words "I don't know," when asking a question of someone who passes for a Customer Service representative. The more knowledgeable you become, the more helpful you will be to others. It isn't enough to smile and look good. Being knowledgeable is the added value that you bring to your Customer Service.

Initiative
Initiative is having the resourcefulness to see what needs done and accomplishing it before anyone asks. Take the initiative to exceed the expectations of others and you will always have an abundance of customers.

Integrity
Be fair and trustworthy, honest and conscientious, and customers will pay you with their loyalty. Act in accordance with these values and you will build a strong and enduring customer base.

Commitment

Customers demand more than ever before. Only individuals with commitment will meet those demands. Do what you say you will do or alert people when you can't. Those who commit to the job, work from the heart.

———

A successful business is about principles, not profits. Get the principles right. The profits will follow.

———

How to Get the Most Out of This Book

You will best absorb the ideas in this book, by reading two or three chapters at a time.

If you read the book straight through, I encourage you to go back and re-read it with a highlighter at hand to mark the ideas that are most important to you. This book will then serve you as a reference manual.

The "Plug in" symbol at the end of a chapter indicates the action, or "take away" point for each chapter.

PHASE 1
Innovation

Customers are always looking for the "Next Big Thing." Stay fresh and relevant in today's rapidly changing business landscape by bringing constant innovation to your organization.

IT'S SHOWTIME!

Do what you do so well that they will want to see it again and bring their friends.   -Walt Disney

SHAKESPEARE was right. The world *is* a stage and if you're in Customer Service, you are the one performing.

So you think Customer Service is strictly business?

Think again!

Tell a customer your company offers quality, service and price and you're likely to get a reply of "BORRRRing! Who doesn't?"

Your customer already knows your price. It's on the Internet. She expects quality to be included at no extra charge. She knows amazing Customer Service when she sees it and frankly, she thinks yours will fall somewhere between "mediocre and atrocious."

SO WHAT?

Today's Customer demands quality, service and price to be already in place. That's the benchmark, the bare minimum, the entry level and if you don't meet that standard from the very beginning, you will constantly be struggling to keep up with those who are perceptive enough to embrace this reality.

WHAT CUSTOMERS WANT
An auto dealer took out a full-page advertisement and printed the testimonial of a satisfied customer as the headline for the ad. It simply read, "It was the best buying experience I ever had." That was it. She didn't say, "It was the cheapest deal in town." Nor, did she give praises about the wonderful features of the new vehicle. She didn't even mention the model she purchased. She simply said it was the best buying experience she ever had.

Most customers are exactly like her. They want an Amazing Customer Experience. Today's customer is accustomed to being entertained.

IT'S NOT THE BIG MAC ®
McDonald's does an excellent job of creating an Amazing Customer Experience. You've probably seen the commercials that play to our focus on family values. The camera drops in on an average family, Mom and Dad with their young children, gathered around red plastic tables for some good old-fashioned family fun. They are all laughing and enjoying their "Happy Meals." If you blink, you might miss the five-seconds of footage highlighting the burgers and fries.

Of course, in the "real world," if the camera dropped in on my family, the kids wouldn't even be at the table. They'd be in Play Land and their mom would be shouting, "Get over here and eat your chicken nuggets before they get cold!" And if the children did happen to be sitting at the table, they would be yelling stuff like, "Mom, he's touching my fries," or "Ooh, yuck, it has onions on it!"

But, the point is, it's not the Big Mac® bringing them in; it's the overall customer experience. The message is, if you want to have a fun night with the family, take them to McDonald's. The food is secondary.

The restaurant and automobile industry aren't the only ones creating a customer experience to sell their product. While Amazon may be the world's largest online bookstore – and by the way, Amazon excels at customer service – the brick and mortar bookstores continue to grow. They offer elaborate settings reminiscent of stylish libraries of the rich and famous. Their interiors, filled with overstuffed chairs and the smell of freshly brewed coffee, invite customers to relax and browse before making their purchase. The bookstores offer something the Internet hasn't yet mastered – an *Amazing Customer Experience*.

If you want to remain relevant in the twenty-first century, you too, need to create for your customers, an Amazing Customer Experience.

———

PLUG IN: Customers buy where they are the most comfortable. Your goal is to make your customer happier after doing business with you than before. Get together with all of your associates and brainstorm some ideas you can use at your business to turn a transaction with your company into an Amazing Customer Experience. Below are some suggestions for jump-starting your brainstorming session.

Engage your customer's senses. What's the first thing a customer sees upon entering your store?

What's the first scent a customer experiences when walking into your business? Is it the smell of burnt coffee, mildew, or an overflowing trash container?

Pay attention to appearances, fragrances and sounds. I know a realtor who lights a vanilla candle in the kitchen of the house she's about to show, twenty minutes before her appointment arrives. She says it creates an inviting scent that engages the customer's imagination by suggesting the aroma of home-cooking and fresh baked goods.

There are several simple things you can do to enhance your environment. Buy an automatic air-freshener. Brew fresh coffee. Light a candle. Take out the trash.

Offer an interactive experience. REI, a retailer who specializes in recreation gear, has simulated outdoor settings – such as a "Rain Room," a climbing rock and bike trail – that are testing stations where members can try out gear before they buy. Golfsmith superstores have practice ranges, classes in custom clubmaking, putting courses and computer analysis of your golf swing. Think of some industry-related interactive ideas for your business and customers will think of you first, when it's time to buy the service or product you sell.

Provide entertainment. Do-It-Yourself centers hold "How-to" demonstrations on everything from how to hang wallpaper to proper paint selection. Barnes and Noble and Borders bookstores provide musical events and feature best-selling authors who lecture and sign books. Here's an inexpensive way you can provide entertainment at your business. Buy a combination

TV/VCR and play product videos or other programs your customers would enjoy.

―――

Create your own Amazing Customer Experience. Be open to new ideas and look at other businesses outside of your trade to see what works for them. Remember to look at your business from the customer's point of view. It's still a people business. People buy from people they like who work at places they enjoy going. Create an Amazing Customer Experience at your business and soon your customers will tell others, "It was the best buying experience I ever had!"

LOOK MOM, NO HANDS!

Some people get credit for being conservative when they are only being stupid.   *– Ken Hubbard*

"IF you could live your life over again, what would you do differently?" Fifty people over the age of 95 answered that question in a study cited by sociologist, Dr. Tony Campolo. Although it drew a variety of answers, a common response shared by almost all was,

"I would risk more."

If the majority of fifty people over the age of ninety-five agreed that they would *risk more* if given the chance, it would seem sound advice for those of us under the age of ninety-five. But, most people are afraid of taking risks, probably because they fear the possibility of failure. Yet, the truth is "playing it safe" isn't any more secure than taking risks.

Taking a risk is taking a chance on a hunch. It involves your intuition, your special insight into something that only you may recognize. That intuitive sense, or gut feeling, is often an indicator that your risk just might pay off. But, if you stop acting on your intuition altogether and insist on verifying every decision you make by facts, then you will find this special sense will soon abandon you altogether. And life will become as dreary and unexciting as it has for poor Hugh.

WHAT HAPPENED TO HUGH?
When Hugh was young, taking risks was the daily routine. He rode his bike with "no hands," climbed impossible trees, and jumped out of his swing at dizzying altitudes.

Then as Hugh grew older, and presumably wiser, he became more cautious. Caution turned into fear. Fear turned into paralysis. Hugh didn't ask a girl to the prom because he was afraid she might say, "No." He turned down the chance to play his drums in the school talent show, because he feared he might make a fool of himself. Hugh was scared of being wrong, getting hurt or falling short.

Hugh decided the best way to avoid risk was to blend with the crowd – to fit in. He hid the parts of his character that were unique and invented a personality that he thought to be acceptable to everyone. Brilliance became blandness.

Perhaps you've seen Hugh. He's the bank teller you've been going to for five years who still thinks your name is, "Next!" He's the waiter who shrugs when you ask about the specials. He's the service manager, who makes you feel like an interruption, the doctor who seems disinterested in your concerns, the person behind the counter with the vacant look who says, "nope, your order's not ready," and offers no time frame for when it might be.

So, why am I telling you about Hugh in a book on customer service? Well, as you've probably guessed, because "Hugh" just might be "You." When you grow comfortable and indifferent. When you slide into a rut and forget to pull yourself out. When you enter into the *Complacency Zone,* you become like Hugh.

It's time to get out – to get uncomfortable. Time to wake up and leave the zone. Start by bringing all of *you* to work. It takes risk to show your true self. But, that is what customers want to see. They've seen glitz and glamour. Now they want to see the "real thing." They want to see you.

———

PLUG IN: There are probably some areas of your life that you're putting on hold because you're afraid of the risk involved. Below are three steps to shake off your complacency, and take the opportunities afforded by risk.

1. **Aim high.** Pursue opportunities that you think are beyond you. Take a risk on the long shot. Even if you reach for something and miss, you've at least begun to stretch and grow.

2. **Leave the Complacency Zone.** Go outside your business, your circle of friends and your regular contacts to explore new worlds. New friends often lead to new opportunities. One of the best ways to get new ideas is from other industries.

3. **Invest in yourself.** Take a risk on you. Spend some time and money on your education. Look

for training opportunities. Attend seminars. Read the top three business or professional development books.

Our survey group of 95 year olds said they would risk more, if given the chance. They probably weren't referring to bungee jumping and parachuting, but to calculated risks backed by a solid action plan. These risks lead to improved opportunities.

Sometimes you may be wrong and sometimes your risks may not pay off. Undoubtedly, you will have to make sacrifices. But in the end, your rewards will outweigh the consequences.

VALUE IS IN THE EYES OF THE CUSTOMER

Value in a service or product is not what you put into it. It is what the client or customer gets out of it.
– Peter Drucker

It's only valuable if your customer says it is. Many businesses miss the point. They spend millions of dollars to add value to a product or a service only to discover they've added something that isn't valuable in the least to the Customer.

We know our product and service so well that we are constantly looking for ways to improve it – in our eyes. It's easy to forget that customers aren't as familiar with our products as we are and their idea of what's valuable can be completely different from ours. The best way to find out what your customers value in the way of service or product features is to *ask them*.

DEFINING VALUE

According to Roy H. Williams, author of *The Wizard of Ads*, "value, in the eyes of the customer, is simply the difference between the anticipated price and the marked price."

In other words, if the customer expects something to cost more than what she pays, it is a "good value." On the other hand, when she pays more than what she expects something to cost, it is "highway robbery."

Sitting at a table across from the regional manager of several nationally known cafeterias, I heard a story that illustrates this point.

I had ordered fish on my trip through the serving line and the manager commented on my selection.

"How's the tilapia?" he asked.

"It's wonderful. Kind of a surprise to see it in your serving line."

"Thanks. What did you think of the price?"

"Oh, $7.99? Can't beat it."

"Yeah, I don't think you can, either. You know, that six-ounce filet costs me six bucks. It's a good value for my customer. But, you know Mia's, that 5 star restaurant downtown where all the celebrities go? I happen to know they buy that very same fish, and they sell it for $32.00! How do they get away with that?"

I thought it would be rude to point out to him the obvious differences between his cafeteria and that of a 5 star restaurant – that Mia's has elegant décor, two international chefs, and professional servers who present the food to your table, not to mention the possibility of those celebrity sightings.

"So what," I could imagine him saying, "If I can save 25 bucks, I'll get my own plate of food,"

But, what he doesn't understand is that it's more than the difference between going through a serving line and having a plate of food brought to your table. There are unseen expenses that drive up the cost of products or services. For instance, Mia's has included in the price of that thirty-two dollar fish, the salaries of two chefs, the expense of the décor, the cost of linen service and a multitude of other amenities that add to the overall customer experience. It's actually a bargain in those terms – *a good value.*

Value isn't simply an artificially inflated price based on the customer's willingness to pay. It's the cost of the extras that are added to a service or product – the value added features.

VALUE YOU CAN SEE

Once you establish a value added framework, document it in such a way that it can be measurable. For example, determine the percentage of your order fill rate and work on improving it. Calculate the number of "perfect orders" that you fill. Assign a time length to your delivery window. In other words, if possible, translate your value-added service into dollars and cents, or time saved, in a way that is meaningful to your customer.

Many people in sales assume that the customer will notice and appreciate valuable service. The truth is, although customers know bad service when they receive it, few customers realize when someone's gone out of their way to deliver great service. Service is often "invisible." That is why it's a good idea to translate service value into time or money saved.

If you deliver something on Tuesday that's not due until Thursday, tell the customer. If you've cross-referenced your customer's part numbers so that they print out on the packing slip and the invoice, let them know about it. When you save the customer money on a product substitution or a freight charge, tell them in dollars and cents.

In his book, *Selling the Invisible,* author Harry Beckwith warns, "Don't expect your customer to see how hard you've worked, how much you have cared, and how well you have performed. So often, the customer is the last to know."

No matter what stories you've heard otherwise, most people *will* pay more for a product or service that they perceive has extra value for them. Few people buy on price alone.

For instance, look at the clothes you wear. Did you buy that shirt or blouse because it was absolutely the cheapest thing you could find? What about your favorite restaurant? Do you go there because it's the cheapest food in town? Most likely, you go there for the overall dining experience.

WHERE EVERYBODY KNOWS YOUR NAME

My wife, Frances, and I go to a small Italian restaurant called Sorge's almost every week. It isn't the price of the food that draws us there. We go there because the staff at Sorge's offers an Amazing Customer Experience.

As soon as we walk in the door, Angela takes our beverage order and Peggy greets us by name as she seats us at "our table." Next, our server, Neda, brings a folded up table cloth to drape across the back of Frances' chair so she'll have a "cushion" when she leans back. Chef Brent Williams personalizes our entrées to suit our taste preferences. In other words, the people at Sorge's spoil us.

During our meal, owners David and Gary Sorge stop by to ask what else can be done to make our experience more enjoyable. The efforts of the entire staff, as well as the atmosphere of the restaurant, combine to provide a remarkable dining experience.

By the way, David and Gary took a risk when they started the restaurant that bears their name. They renovated an old building that originally was a pizza place. During a ten-year span, four businesses moved into the building, only to move out again. Then the Sorges moved in.

Where others failed, Gary and David succeeded by using this little formula: Let the customer tell you what value is and then determine how you can exceed it.

 PLUG IN: Promise small. Deliver big. Here are three ways that will take you FAR in adding value to your business proposition.

1. **Focus**. Focus more on your Customer's business than you do on yours or your competitors'. Customize a solution for an individual client and you could have a Customer for Life.

2. **Ask!** Ask your customer what services they would like to see in a supplier. Is it

shorter delivery time, more diverse product line, deeper inventory? Don't assume to know what your customer values.

3. **Research.** Research your customers' business challenges and problems. Find ways you can help solve them. Earn a reputation as a solution supplier, not a product pusher.

Add services that your customer deems valuable – and then let them know about it. Help your customer see that you are making a significant contribution to making their business run smoother.

COMPETING WITH A MOUSE

Service that does not jump to meet the rising expectations [of customers] will have...a customer exodus on its hands.
— Harry Beckwith

You may think your competitors are the companies and organizations who sell the same products or services as you.

No way.

You are competing against a number of companies who aren't at all like you.

You're competing with Federal Express who can deliver a package overnight anywhere in the United States for less than thirty bucks.

You're competing with McDonald's who can deliver America's favorite fries in less than a minute.

You're competing with Disney who holds weekly staff meetings on "Guest courtesy." (Disney calls their customers, "Guests," with a capitol G.)

These are just a few of the businesses who have redefined Customer Service for the entire world. They, and the others like them, are responsible for raising customer's expectations. These organizations changed the landscape of Customer Service.

Also, understand you are competing against a number of alternatives. It's fruitless to pinpoint a competitor and focus on what that one business is doing. In fact, it's best to *spend as little time as possible* thinking about your competition. You want people to perceive you as being different in a way that appeals to your customer, not as a carbon copy of your competition.

Your focus needs to be on solving your client's problems with customized solutions for each individual need. Spend time discovering business needs and how you can contribute in a significant way. If you can do that, you won't have to worry about the competition. There won't be any.

———

 PLUG IN: Instead of shrugging your shoulders and asking, "What can I do to complete with these world-class companies?" remember this: an individual just like you started each one.

Here is a three-step plan to start you on your way to delivering world-class service to your customers.

1. List two or three companies you admire for their excellent service.

2. Write down one thing you can adapt from their service that will enhance yours.

3. Outline the steps you will need to take to adapt these ideas to your business. Take action.

MAKE IT EASY

In business, you get what you want by giving other people what they want. *– Alice MacDougall*

"This is an emergency. A plant has a production line down and it's costing, like a $1000.00 a minute, or something. What's the fastest way I can get this product shipped out?" I asked.

"You can call one of our distributors or you can order online. *Or* you can place the order with me and I'll ship it out today, overnight delivery, and you'll have it tomorrow. Which do you prefer?"

"We don't even have an account with you."

"You will after you place your order."

This was not typical of my experience with manufacturers. Usually, a manufacturer insists you call the distributor in your area. If the distributor doesn't have the product then they have to order it from the manufacturer, thus adding another step to the process and increasing the likelihood that somewhere along the way, something will go wrong. Some manufacturers will only ship directly to the distributor and that adds another day until the product reaches your door.

This vendor made it easy for me to order from her. She didn't waste my time with any type of protocol nonsense. She simply said, "You need our product. Let us make it as easy as possible for you to buy it."

IF I HAD A HAMMER

Recently, I hired a carpenter to make some modifications to our sales counter. Most of our expenses are handled with a purchasing card, which is simply a credit card designed for use by corporations. In the past two years, I've seen a growth of these cards used by our customers, as well.

When the carpenter invoiced us for the work he had done, I offered to pay with the company-purchasing card. He wasn't set up to take credit cards—cash or checks only. Our company only issues checks from the corporate office. Corporate requires two separate forms filled out before issuing a check to cover an expense. The process can take two weeks when everything goes well. In this instance, a miscommunication caused a month delay before the check arrived.

Five weeks later, after numerous calls to me, the carpenter received his check. Had he been set up to take credit cards he would've received his money in twenty-four hours. Even with the percentage that the credit card companies charge for their service, he would receive a better return on his money than he did waiting five weeks for his money. And that doesn't even account for the time he wasted calling me.

We will probably never use his services again, because it's too inconvenient to do business with him. That's an even bigger loss than the return on receiving his money faster.

———

Plug in: Do you make customers go through a long, drawn out process to set up an account? Do you require tedious detailed information before you will sell a customer your product or service?

"But, I've got to check a prospects credit, don't I?"

Of course you do. But, you can be efficient and timely about it. For instance, do you really need the prospect to list all of his creditors when you're going to pull a credit report that's going to list them anyway?

An individual with a so-so credit rating can go into an auto dealer and drive out with a $40,000 automobile in about an hour. You can get a $5000 line of credit at most department stores while you wait in line. Why would you expect a customer to wait longer for you to process her credit, just for the privilege of having an account with you?

- Take credit cards, or create your own prepaid cash cards that customers can use in your store or online.

- Streamline your credit department. Stop asking the customer to provide information that you can get yourself.

- Make it as easy as possible for your clients to buy. Offer multiple channels for your customer to do business with you.

If you don't make it easy for your customers to buy, you can lose a prospect without even knowing it – like my carpenter friend. His only memory of our company will be how hard it was for him to do business with us and he's probably thinking, "Man, I'll never do business with them again."

He's right, but he's missing the point. He needs to be thinking of ways to make it easier for customers to do business with him, not the other way around. He'll never know the business he's losing until he learns to *make it easy*.

KNOW THY CUSTOMER

IF you read any type of business magazine, you've probably seen the ads for CRM. Most of them don't even tell you what the initials stand for, but make bold promises about how it could triple your sales, manage your time more efficiently and take 3 strokes off your golf game.

So what is it?

Kate O'Sullivan in the April 2001 issue of *Inc.* defined it this way.

> Customer-Relationship Management, or **CRM,** refers broadly to all aspects of marketing, sales and service that pertain to customers. More narrowly, it describes a software-based system that manages the information a business gathers about its customers.

The gathered information can include data about each one of your clients down to the tiniest detail. For example, when I phone in a to-go order to Pizza Hut, they can tell me what toppings I like on my pizza, my crust preference, and the names of each of my children. After a driver got lost once on the way to our address, they even keyed in the shortcut to my home. (Scary!)

You can record purchasing activity, buying trends, names of children, golf handicap and any other information that will help you become more familiar with each person you serve. The reasoning behind this, of course, is that the better you know your client the better your relationship can become.

CRM is not some revolutionary new idea, as the hype would lead you to believe. It is simply a repackaging of a timeless Customer Service concept: the more you know your customer, the more you can serve his needs.

Our Executive VP reminded us of that recently. Several of us were pushing our company to adopt a CRM software program for each sales rep. When we extolled the virtues of what this program could do to provide us with a detailed database, he said, "You act like this is something new. When I was a salesman, I created my own Customer Relationship Management program and computers weren't even around. I built a database using a yellow legal pad and a #2 pencil!"

I know that sounds like one of those "when I was your age" stories your parents told about walking to school in the snow, but he has a point. Yes, I do believe you need to invest in CRM software that suits your needs. But, if you're not already managing your client base in some way, having a software program won't suddenly make you start building one. You still need the discipline to gather the information and enter it into your database.

This brings up another point. Not having a fancy database program doesn't excuse you from building profiles on your customers. Even if you think you can't afford, or won't use, a software program, you can always do what our EVP did. Use a yellow legal pad and a #2 pencil and some type of filing system. The biggest advantage to one of the CRM programs is the ease of access it allows you to search out and find information.

PLUG IN: At the entrance elevators to Estee Lauder's headquarters in Manhattan, is a green glass plaque with the company motto engraved: *Bringing the best to everyone we touch.* Estee Lauder understood that the business of selling something as personal as cosmetics required a personal relationship with each customer.

If you don't already have a database of clients, start building one today. "Start where," you ask? With the next person you meet. That's right. That's the beauty of a database. Everyone you know has a place in it. With a customer relationship management program, you can:

- Keep track of birthdays and special occasions
- Jump-start conversations
- Ask about someone's family members by name
- Track purchase history
- Set reminders for upcoming events

Wouldn't you be a better conversationalist if you had background information on the people you know that would enable you to ask about their kids, or a new job or project, or hobby? You could even ask about their dog, Punky.

A customer relationship management program is an ongoing process – a project that doesn't end. Once you start to develop one, the momentum will motivate you to imagine new ways to put it to use.

The point is Customer Service doesn't end at your place of business. It is a frame of mind, an attitude that becomes who you are: a person who serves others. And the better at it you become, the more you will find that the world serves you in return.

JUST SAY YES!

THEY'RE gone!
Did you notice?
Those signs outside of mall stores that read:

NO FOOD OR DRINK ALLOWED IN THIS STORE

I'm not sure when they were removed. I just noticed one day that they were gone and I suspect I know why. Because some brilliant marketing genius had a light bulb moment one day and said, "Hey! You know the first word a customer sees before they walk into our store? The word 'NO.' And that's the invitation we give our customer to come in and buy something."

The signs disappeared over night. All of the major department stores must have gotten the word at the same time because once they were gone from one, they were gone from all.

> *"Well, I don't have one of those signs outside my business. So, what's this got to do with me?"*

Okay, so maybe you don't have the sign outside your building but I'll bet you have it *inside*. If you've ever told a customer, *no, we don't have that,* or *no, we can't do that,* then you might as well wear a sign around your neck with the word "NO" in four-inch letters.

Ask yourself this question, "Do I like to hear the word, 'N-O.'"

Well, neither do your customers.

But what do I say, if I can't provide what they want?

Easy. Tell them what you **can** provide.

This little scenario always amazes me every time I go with my wife to a shoe store and she asks for a shoe in her size. When the sale person comes out empty handed, Frances asks, "Do you have a half-size smaller or larger?" Most of the time they'll return from the stock room with one or both sizes. Did you know there's only a 1/8 inch difference in most half sizes? Apparently, neither do most shoe salespeople. I can't count the number of times my wife has sold the shoe *for* the salesperson by suggesting they go back and look again – for another size, another color, another style.

But, won't the customer think I'm just trying to sell them something.

Yes, and that's why they showed up in the first place – so that you would try to sell them something. And, here's what they think if you *don't* make an effort to sell something else – that you don't care or that you're just plain lazy.

Well, that's fine for shoes, but what about when you don't have anything close to what the customer wants?

Then that's when you get creative. A customer once came to our sales counter for a 175 metal-halide lamp. Bruce, a guy who hates to tell a customer *no*, already knew we were out of the lamp, but he went to the warehouse anyway. A moment later, he reappeared holding a complete new light fixture.

"I just wanted the bulb," the customer protested.

Bruce answered, "I know. But, when I saw that we didn't have it, I figured what you really needed was the light." Bruce grinned and held up the fixture. "So, I brought you a light."

The customer laughed at Bruce's determination and bought the fixture. I think he bought it just because he was impressed that Bruce went out of his way to keep from saying, "No, we don't have that."

There's always an alternative to saying, "NO."

―――

PLUG IN: If you work with associates, challenge them to catch you saying, "No," to a customer. Tell them you'll pay a quarter each time you say it. (If you are already in the habit of saying N-O quite a bit, then maybe you should start with a dime).

Remember, no one likes to hear the word "No." Be creative as you think of alternatives to a negative response and encourage your co-workers to combine resources with you in your efforts to drop the word "NO" from your vocabulary,

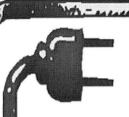

PHASE 2 Commitment

Commitment means doing what you say you will do or alerting people when you can't. Those who commit to providing amazing Customer Service work from the heart.

TURNING CUSTOMERS INTO PROSPECTS

If you work as hard to keep my business as you do to earn my business, then you will always have my business. –George Hester

THE red blazer ambassadors from the Chamber of Commerce are all present. The district manager and several people from the marketing department have flown in to witness the big event. The manager and the employees of the new business are all smiles and enthusiasm. Customers gather, anticipating, "This is the store we've been waiting for – the one with the right products at an affordable price backed up with great Customer Service."

The manager cuts the ribbon and customers pour into the store. Shaking hands, exchanging names, amid sounds of laughter makes this a day to celebrate commerce at its best!

Truly, this is a ***Grand*** Opening! What a tremendous success! The business' corporate execs are thrilled. The manager and her new staff are excited and keep up a high level of energy until closing time, eleven hours later. Reluctantly, they watch the last customers leaving the store ten minutes *after* closing time.

FAST-FORWARD

Six months later. It's hard to tell the employees from the customers. Their facial expressions are blank. A cashier listlessly scans a customer's items and ends the transaction with a barely audible "That be all?"

The manager rushes across the store to answer a phone call, ignoring customers in her path. A prerecorded voice over the intercom announces that the store will be closing in twelve minutes and customers should bring their purchases to a register. The countdown continues every two minutes, each announcement with an underlying message to *just buy something and get out of the store! NOW!*

What happened?

What happened to the excitement, the laughter, the friendliness? Where did the neatly dressed personnel with the enthusiastic smiles and warm handshakes disappear?

Complacency set in. On its opening day, a business has no customers. It only has *prospects* for customers. Once the business wins over the prospect – turns them into customers – then most sales people perceive the challenge to be over.

But, here's the real challenge: how do you maintain the level of energy and excitement that you have when you are trying to turn a prospect into a customer? The answer is, "Keep thinking of your customers as prospects." You have to win them over every time they enter into your place of business.

When I started in sales, I spent a lot of time and energy chasing one of the biggest manufacturers in town. Our competition "owned" the account. The loyalty between the two companies was the result of years of growing together. I was determined to make an impact on that relationship.

Finally, I was able to secure an appointment with the Vice President of Plant Operations, George Hester. He was a straightforward man of authority. He was not concerned about old loyalties and "good ol' boy" relationships. He was driven only by what best served the company.

I delivered my presentation. I used flip charts, graphs and testimonials. I shared our finest brochures, our best success stories and photos of my children. I sang. I danced. I cried.

George Hester was unmoved; his expression, poker-faced, his mood somber and questioning. Finally, with the slightest hint of a smile, he said, "You know, Mike, I used to be a salesman. I sold fasteners; nuts and bolts. It took me five years of persistence and hard work to land my biggest account, but I always knew it would be worth it. And I'll never forget the first decent order I got from the owner and what he said after he issued me a purchase order. I reached for the order and he held on to it after I grabbed it. He stared at me, both of us holding this single piece of paper as if we were about to have a tug of war. It must have been half a minute before he spoke. Then he said, 'Son, if you work as hard to keep my business as you did to earn my business, then you will always have my business.' And now that's what I'm telling you. *Earn my business.*"

Eventually, I did earn the business, but the challenge faces each of us every day – to work as hard to keep the business.

We work hard to win over a prospect – to turn them into a customer – then we place them in a "maintenance" file in our brains and are off to chase down the next one. Those who achieve remarkable success will be the ones who are able to continue to show the same level of enthusiasm and energy to their existing customers as they do their prospects.

 PLUG IN: Think of each day as "Opening Day." You have no customers until they walk into your place of business and buy something.

Remember at the beginning of the day that you have a new opportunity to create, deepen, and enhance your Customer Service. See each transaction with an existing customer for what it really is; something unique that has never happened before.

When a customer first makes eye contact, brighten your expression and bring a smile to your face as if you're seeing a friend for the first time in years.

Practice George Hester's rule:

Work as hard to keep my business as you do to earn my business and you will always have my business.

JUST A NOTE TO SAY "THANKS"

Gratitude costs nothing, but it's a big investment in your future. – Napoleon Hill

LIKE most people, Jerry doesn't say "thank you" often enough. Indeed, he hardly says it at all. He asks Pam to volunteer to serve on a committee that requires three hours of her leisure time each week. He has Joe to come speak to his civic club about business ethics. Joe spends six hours putting the presentation together and another two hours to be at the meeting. Jerry asks his preacher, Reverend Simpson, to write a letter of recommendation so that he may qualify for membership in a professional association. Richard spends an hour writing the document.

When Pam and Joe and Reverend Simpson have completed their volunteer assignments, they hear nothing from Jerry. No phone call. No casual, "thanks," as they pass by him in the hall. Nothing. Nada. Zilch.

Jerry *is* grateful for all the help he receives from others and he thinks that they feel his gratitude. He doesn't know what he would do without the help of people gracious enough to volunteer their time. But no one knows it, because he never says it.

What about you? How often do you say, "Thanks"? When was the last time you said a sincere "thank you –"

- to the buyer who gave you the order when your competitor was less expensive?
- to a busy co-worker for assisting you with a project?
- to the assistant who compiled and submitted your proposal?

Did you just think they already knew you were grateful?

Remember, also, to be thankful to those who are closest to you – family and friends who support and encourage you. Chances are that because you are so close, you take for granted that they know how you feel about them. They probably do, but gratitude expressed in words is more meaningful and true to life.

To excel in business you need to stand out from the crowd. You need to avoid conformity and look for ways to set yourself apart from everyone else in your industry. Now that so many people rely almost exclusively on email for written communication, the custom of writing thank you notes is almost gone. And that's why you should do it. Because you will stand out from the crowd and be remembered.

Sociologists tell us that the last impression you make on another individual is the one they are most likely to remember. What better last impression can you leave than to show your gratitude for something someone else has done?

PLUG IN: Make your gratitude work for you. Be creative. Develop a habit of sending out a thank you note or card once a week. Here is a format for writing a thank you note for a client, colleague or vendor.

> **Dear Ed Hensley,**
>
> I want to express my sincere thanks for the time you spent with me on Tuesday, discussing our new product line.
>
> I enjoyed visiting with you and found your remarks very helpful. I think there are several areas where our products will be beneficial to your company.
>
> It's always a pleasure to work with you and if you have any follow up concerns, please call me at 555-778-2808 or send email to: ss@widget.com
>
> Regards,
> Steven Scott

Send a note to thank the client who adjusts his schedule to listen to your latest sales presentation. Send one to thank the buyer even when you aren't the successful bidder. Send one when you get the order or win the bid. Send another thanking them for their patronage, their assistance, their forgiveness when your company makes a mistake.

Send a note of congratulations when your customer wins an award or appears in the media. It will surprise your customer. You will set yourself apart from your competitors. You will improve your rapport with your client and you will gain an advantage in the close deals – and maybe in the ones that aren't even close.

How to Deal With Difficult Customers

Customer complaints are the schoolbooks from which we learn.   *- Unknown*

No matter how good your Customer Service is, there will always be someone who is unhappy about something. In fact, some people aren't happy *unless* they're unhappy. They are constantly looking for a flaw in your service and will take advantage of your policies by making requests that sometimes border on the absurd. *And* they will teach you how to deliver amazing Customer Service. You can learn more from the difficult customer than you could ever learn from your most loyal. Difficult customers tell you where it hurts.

    If you listen, they will tell you what is missing from your business and might even suggest what you can do about it. Their feedback can be the most honest gauge of your success.

    If you have an abundance of difficult customers, it's not because you're unlucky. It's because you're doing something wrong. The sooner you figure out what it is and fix it, the sooner you will bring your business back from the precipice of disaster.

True, there will be an occasional customer who has no valid reason to complain, but complains anyway. Be able to discern the legitimate complaint from the absurd demand.

PLUG IN: Handling difficult customers may be your biggest challenge in delivering an Amazing Customer Experience. Having a procedure in place for all of your staff to follow is the most effective way to handle this challenge. Here is a suggested four-step plan that may be helpful for dealing with the legitimate customer complaint.

1. Never argue. *Let me repeat that*, because it seems to be the toughest one for people to accept. NEVER ARGUE. Even if you win, you lose. Especially if you win.

2. LISTEN between the lines. Is there an underlying message to your customer's complaint? Does he feel cheated, ignored or unappreciated?

3. Appeal to your customer's nobler motives – her sense of fair play. Let the customer know that you trust her enough to do what's fair and right. A question you can use that takes the fire out of most irate customers is, "What would you have me do to make this right?" If you appeal to a customer's nobler motives, most of the time she will live up to your expectation.

4. Tell the customer what you can do. Never say, "That's against company policy." (If someone in authority within your company tells you to say that, then you need to reconsider your career with that company). Suggest alternatives. Keep your temper. Above all, let your customer save face.

THE MAGIC OF 30

Getting people to like you is only the other side of liking them. Norman Vincent Peale

As far back as I can remember I received a birthday card every year from a man I never met. Inside the card, there was always a stick of gum. One year I asked my mom, "Who is this guy?"

She said, "He's just some salesman that tried to sell us insurance."

"Tried to?"

"Yes. Your father already had insurance and didn't buy any from him."

"So he's sent these birthday cards all these years to the son of a man who didn't buy his insurance?"

"That's right."

Now that's amazing. I'd like to give the story a happy ending and tell you that when I grew up, I bought insurance from him. I didn't.

But, this salesman obviously had a very organized system for developing prospects and knew about Customer Relationship Management long before the term was coined. Although, no one in my family ever spent a dime with him, I'm sure the man's business flourished because of this one little campaign alone.

STAY WITHIN 30 DAYS

Years later, I met a business consultant by the name of Mark LeBlanc who wrote a book called, *Growing Your Business*. Mark shared a suggestion from his book that reminded of the persistent insurance salesman who never forgot my birthday.

Here is Mark's elaborately simple idea:

Make a list of your top thirty customers.
Contact each one of them every thirty days.

Contact includes email, phone, letter or card or any other way you can come up with to let them know they are never far from your thoughts. Everyone likes to feel important. With the deluge of spam, junk mail and bills, people love a personal contact from someone who doesn't want anything more than to say hello.

Of course, cynics will say, "But, you *do* want something from them."

Absolutely. You do.

You want their friendship and their well-being. You want for their health and happiness. And yes, when the time comes, you want their consideration when purchasing your product or service.

 PLUG IN: To stagger your method of contacting individuals, you can use the following schedule from Mark LeBlanc's book, *Growing Your Business*.

Jan – Make a Happy New Year phone call
Feb – Send an info sheet about your business
Mar – Mail an advertisement
Apr – Forward an article from a trade magazine
May – Send a postcard
Jun – Email a note
Jul – Face-to-Face visit
Aug – Fax a note
Sep – Send a company newsletter
Oct – Mail early holiday card
Nov – Call again
Dec – Your choice from above

As you can see, all of the above will cost you less than five dollars per customer. Not bad for a year long marketing campaign. If you want to get really creative and invest another fifty dollars, throw in a five dollar gift card to your top ten for their birthday or holiday.

The key to the success of this program is to keep it simple and light, so that you don't miss a month. Consistency is the main ingredient in the recipe for an Amazing Customer Experience. Do this and you will build a roster of loyal customers who will honor you with their business and with their referrals.

WHEN BAD THINGS HAPPEN TO GOOD CUSTOMERS

Customers don't expect you to be perfect. They do expect you to fix things when they go wrong.
- Donald Porter V.P., British Airways

MARK is a local celebrity in his city. When his "big sister" and her husband visit, Mark likes to treat them to dinner in a fancy, lavish five star restaurant. On one occasion, upon arriving at the restaurant of choice, Mark and his family learned there were no reservations in his name. He calmly asked, "Well, what are we going to do fix this? I'm sure there's something your manager can do."

The maître d' returned with the manager, who apologized for the error and assured Mark they would resolve the situation at once. Meanwhile, the maître d' went to several tables and explained to each diner that the restaurant had misplaced a reservation and asked if they would mind helping by allowing their table to be slightly "shifted." He offered them a twenty percent discount off their bill for their inconvenience. Naturally, the customers complied.

A space cleared in the middle of the room and four waiters carried in a table and chairs. In less than three minutes, accommodations were ready for Mark and his family.

Sooner or later, you're going to disappoint a customer. How you handle that crisis, will determine whether you lose a patron or gain a devoted supporter. If you can make a customer feel special after you've disappointed them, you've taken a negative situation and transformed it into a positive.

———

PLUG IN: When you make a mistake, make no excuses. Own the mistake and begin to correct it at once. However, it doesn't do you or your associates any good if you try to solve a problem without a specific plan. The following steps offer a blueprint for crisis resolution that you can adapt to your business. This guide comes from the book, *Juiced!* by Lipkin and Gillis.

1. Apologize immediately with genuine empathy. [The manager apologized to Mark without restraint for the embarrassment and inconvenience the misplaced reservation caused his family.]

2. Take responsibility. Take control. Don't badmouth your company and don't go hunting for blame in front of the Customer. Dance, Don't Fight. [The manager didn't come out with blazing accusations saying, "It's the hostess' fault!" *He* took the heat. He *owned* the problem and made no

excuses. Your customer doesn't care who's to blame.]

3. Do whatever you can to fix the problem or resolve the situation immediately. Be crisis-ready. [The manager had extra tables and chairs for just such an emergency.]

4. Have a resource-in-reserve that can be applied when and where it's needed fast. [The manager authorized the twenty percent discount to the other diners to express gratitude at their willingness to help. You might keep gift cards to give to Customers to offset the bitterness of a disappointment – along with an apology.]

5. Minimize the Customer's inconvenience or discomfort financially, emotionally and physically. Take the sting out of the negative experience. Manage your customer's memory. [Will Mark remember the misplaced reservation or the way they fixed it? Both, but he won't tell the story without telling what they did to alleviate the problem.]

6. Follow up within 24 hours. Make another deposit into the memory bank account. [Mark received a thank you note for his patronage and for his patience and understanding along with another apology for the inconvenience.]

7. Evaluate the service delivery process and implement changes to prevent the mistake happening again. "What can we learn from this?"

Only you can answer the last question. Adapt and apply this guide as needed. In fact, you don't need to save it for your customers. You can adapt it to work with family and friends, too. Run towards a problem, not away from it.

"A crisis is a moment of truth: you can make it a moment of magic or a moment of misery."

Follow Up

Think things through – then follow through.
—Eddie Rickenbacker

FOLLOW up can make a bigger difference than almost any other aspect of Customer Service.

Why?

Because so few people do it. Think about the last time someone followed up with you. Did it make an impression?

Follow up begins after the customer's initial contact with you. It may take the form of simply calling to thank a customer for an order.

The most critical part of follow up is keeping a commitment. When you promise to check on an order, remember to do get back to your client with an answer. If you say you will send an item to the client's office, be sure you send it.

As your clientele grows, it becomes necessary to develop a system for following up and keeping commitments.

When you follow up you are letting customers know that your service continues after the sale. It is another way of providing value.

Plug in: Here are some suggestions for organizing your efforts to provide amazing follow up.

- **Carry a planner:** There are several excellent brands of schedulers in many convenient formats. These organizers have calendars and timelines you can use to keep track of your commitments to customers.

- **Make a daily to-do list.** Take the time to write down the immediate tasks you need to accomplish each day. Even if you never look at the list again, unconsciously you will begin to take care of the items on it. Many times when I don't think I have time to make a list, I'll create one anyway. Later, I'm always surprised when I see how many of the items can be crossed off at the end of the day.

- **Use a PDA**. A Personal Data Assistant works great with a CRM program. However, this system works best if you consider yourself highly computer literate.

"Plays Well With Others"

In a shopping mall, I recently passed by someone wearing a T-shirt that had the words, "DOESN'T PLAY WELL WITH OTHERS" in three-inch block letters across the front. I thought it was funny. But, when you have a coworker who seems to have those words tattooed across his forehead, it's no laughing matter.

Lee Iacocca said, "The statement, 'He's good, but he has trouble getting along with other people,' is the kiss of death for management potential. The major reason capable people fail to advance is that they don't work well with their colleagues and customers."

It really comes down to having a love for people and the ability to show others that you care for their well-being. That means getting along with your coworkers as well as your customers. Why? Because your coworkers are your customers, too.

Say what?

That's right. Even though your coworkers probably don't buy anything from you, they are still your customers—what the business books call, internal customers. Because each individual at a company has the ability to contribute or to take away from the success of the organization, it is important to your success that everyone does an excellent job of customer service. Your coworkers are actually an indirect link between you and the external customer. So, it is important to treat your work associates in the same manner that you treat your customers.

Yeah, but you just don't understand. You don't know the people I have to work with. Is it my fault if my coworker is a jerk?

No, it's not your fault if your coworker is a jerk, but there's always something you can do to influence the performance of others. Understand the interconnectedness between you and every other employee in your company. How well you deal with difficult coworkers will reflect in how well you deal with difficult customers. It is the overall performance of the company that determines its success. Therefore, your fellow employees have an effect on your livelihood.

"Employee satisfaction equals customer satisfaction at UPS," says Kent Nelson, former UPS CEO. The smart companies, the customer-focused companies know this. These companies have figured out that keeping employees happy is the key to keeping customers happy.

PLUG IN: Most bosses still operate from the old mindset, "My employees know if I don't say anything critical about their performance, then that means they're doing a good job. If I compliment an employee all the time, it'll just give him a big head." If you have a boss like that then you know that the only encouragement your coworkers receive will have to come from you or others who are like you.

1. Make sure that you treat your coworkers in the same way you treat your customers; with courtesy, concern and compassion.

2. Catch someone doing something right. Research says that nothing motivates employees more than peer recognition. When you see a coworker going out of their way to serve a customer, offer some enthusiastic encouragement.

3. Exceed the expectations of your coworkers. If your boss needs a report on Tuesday, give it to him Monday afternoon. (Yes, your boss is an internal customer, too). If the credit department needs some information that you have access to, rather than arguing with them over whose job it is, provide the information for them.

If you make a commitment to assist your coworkers and colleagues, they will be eager to assist you when you need their help. Anyone who helps you get your job done contributes to your success.

PHASE 3
Knowledge

The more knowledgeable you become the more helpful you will be to others. Being knowledgeable is the added value that you bring to an Amazing Customer Experience.

THAT'S WHAT I'M TALKING ABOUT!

"What we've got here is failure to communicate."
- Captain, Road Prison 36

THAT line from the movie, ***Cool Hand Luke***, was practically an anthem back in the 60's. It seemed to imply that most of the problems and conflicts of that era resulted from poor communication.

Now forty years later, the ability to communicate effectively is the number one quality that a business looks for when hiring a new employee, according to the U.S. Bureau of Labor.

Why would an employer single this out as the most desirable trait in a worker? Because poor communication is costly. Think of your own experiences. How much money and time have you spent trying to fix a problem caused by miscommunication?

THE HIGH COST OF SILENCE

"But, she didn't tell me how soon she needed it!" Jim protests to a colleague. Jim's customer, Janet Brown, is furious. She's paying for workers who are standing around with nothing to do, because they are waiting for material from Jim.

"I thought she knew it would take seven days," Again Jim tries to justify his mistake by accusing the customer of not telling him how soon she needed the materials on the job. But then, Jim didn't ask, either. Jim realizes he could've avoided this—

- by telling the customer up front how long it would take for the material to ship.

- by asking the customer when materials needed to be on site.

- by suggesting alternative shipping arrangements.

Then Ms. Brown could have made the decision to spend money on overnight service or reschedule the job.

Many sales reps are like Jim. They don't want to tell bad news, or at least what they *think* will be bad news, to the customer.

At the core of a successful business is the ability to communicate well; to put across your identity and what you do, to convey compelling reasons why your customer should buy from you and to connect with associates in order to enlist their cooperation.

Master your communication skills and you will increase the prosperity of your business, improve the morale of your organization and enjoy results that are more productive in all of your personal relationships.

The biggest problem most of us have communicating is that we don't always say what we really mean. We're like the mayor in the old joke about the farmer who attended a political campaign.

> FARMER'S WIFE: "Who spoke at the political rally?"
> FARMER: "The mayor."
> FARMER'S WIFE: "What did he talk about?"
> FARMER: "He didn't say."

We talk around what we are really trying to say. As comedian Fred Allen once said, we walk around backwards so we don't have to face an issue.

 PLUG IN: This one idea could change your life more than any other in this book, and it's probably the one you're least likely to try. One of the best things you can do for your career is to join Toastmasters International. Even if you don't think you need it. *Especially,* if you don't think you need it. If you are so comfortable that you don't get just a little bit nervous when you step in front of an audience, chances are you come across as bored, complacent or arrogant.

Toastmasters International focuses on the development and refinement of leadership and communication skills. At each meeting, you will learn:
- how to speak in front of a group of your peers.
- how to lead meetings and make presentations.
- the latest business trends and marketing skills to assist you in reaching your goals.

Join it, even if you don't think you need it. You will be surrounding yourself with a group of positive new friends all working together in the pursuit of professional development.

Try it for six months and you will see a remarkable change in your ability to connect with other people. Learning to speak effectively in front of groups is one of the fastest ways to boost confidence and raise self-esteem.

You may visit the website for Toastmasters International to locate a club in your area. The web address is www.toastmasters.org.

In this Age of Information, the communicator will be the leader of tomorrow.

READ YOUR CUSTOMER'S MAGAZINES

You may not find them on the newsstand, but these publications may be the most important magazines you can get your hands on. – Stephan Schiffman

ALMOST every lobby has them. Casually scattered across end tables and coffee tables are the magazines that you never see on the newsstand. They all have names that are unfamiliar and often unwieldy, like *The Laminates and Core Resin Products Monthly* and *The Extrusion Express Quarterly*. These magazines aren't in the lobby for the employees to read. They are placed there as a test – a test to see how interested you are in their company.

By picking these magazines up and skimming through the pages, you're showing an interest in the buyer beyond what they can do for you. You are expressing a curiosity about what your customer does.

You are also finding ways to connect with your customer. Perhaps you learn of a trend in their industry. After reading the article about it, you are able to converse beyond the inane small talk that so many reps pass off as sales rhetoric.

Your industry also has magazines. Your employer probably even pays for a subscription. If you read these magazines, you will be setting yourself apart from everyone else in your organization, considering the fact that only between 5-10 percent of Americans read. You will also be aware of the latest industry trends and innovations.

These publications may contain some of the most important information you can find about your customers. Take advantage of this valuable inside resource.

———

 PLUG IN: The next time you see your customer's trade magazines in their lobby, make a point of skimming through them. In fact, if you ask to "borrow one," your customer will probably just give it to you and be delighted you showed an interest.

Sometime you may find a client featured in one of these magazines. How impressive is it to the client when she gets a congratulatory note and the article clipping from you in the mail? (See Chapter 4)

If your company has an industry magazine, subscribe to it. If you tell your employer about your interest, she just might pay the subscription price for you.

Set aside some time each month to read your customers' magazines and you will benefit by being aware of upcoming trends and industry gossip.

THE 2% SOLUTION

BRYAN Tracy encourages people who attend his seminars to commit to improve themselves by two percent per week. The biggest reason people give for not changing is that it's simply too hard to overcome habits developed over a lifetime.

It is unrealistic to believe you can change one hundred percent overnight. But, it isn't unreasonable to set a goal of improving yourself by two per-cent each week.

Self-improvement, or professional development curriculum, isn't just for overachievers anymore. In a world where software versions change each week and computer upgrades render new systems obsolete before they're installed, it's absolutely essential for anyone who wants to stay relevant in today's workforce.

Personal development is about upgrading YOU. It's about becoming responsible for your own career. It's about staying current with – or even more importantly – staying ahead of your industry, your market, your clientele. And believe me, no matter what your career path, it's changing every day. You are responsible for have to keeping up.

"But, my company doesn't pay for that," I hear you whine. It doesn't matter. Remember, you are the

CEO of your company. Your employer is just another client. Besides, you will probably benefit more if you do pay for it.

Attend a seminar, read books and magazines, listen to professional development tapes. Which ones? Any of them. That's right. It makes little difference if you study geometry, learn a new language or take a continuing ed class in auto mechanics. Research indicates that any type of learning stretches the mind.

With the speed of change in the world today, if you don't keep your mind alert and fresh and filled with new information, you will become as obsolete as last year's microchip processor.

"But, I've got years of experience. That ought to count for something."

Yeah, and so do phone booths. How many of those have you seen lately? Your experience is only valuable for the insights it can shed on new and pertinent information.

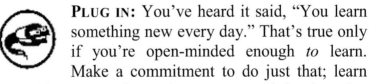

PLUG IN: You've heard it said, "You learn something new every day." That's true only if you're open-minded enough *to* learn. Make a commitment to do just that; learn something new today and tomorrow and the day after that.

Subscribe to an educational magazine like *Discover* or *National Geographic* or a contemporary business magazine like *Fast Company* or *Inc.* These magazines hire reporters and photographers to communicate the most current information and trends.

Take Bryan Tracy's challenge. Commit to improve two percent a week. The effort is minimal. The rewards go beyond financial. You will increase your sense of self-confidence, your value to the human race and your likelihood of a long life.

SAVE THE WORLD AND BE IN BED BY 10:00

When people hear nothing but reports of violent crime day after day, they naturally develop a tremendous sense of fear and anxiety.   –Stephen Kinzer

WHAT was the last thing you watched on TV last night? I'll bet it was the late night news. And what was on? The latest crimes, unemployment and overseas conflicts?

What was the first thing you read this morning? Bet it was the morning news. And what was new? Conflicts and battles, global warming, death and destruction in all parts of the globe?

Were you able to help with any of the world's problems you saw on the news? Did you halt deforestation, bring about peace or see justice served? Was any of the information helpful to you? Or, did it make you feel the world was going to you-know-where in a hand-basket?

We are creatures of habit. We stay up and watch the news before we go to bed, probably because that's what our parents did. And then we go to bed with all of the world's problems still in our heads.

We read the paper in the morning because that's when it comes to our door. On our way to the job, we turn on the radio and listen to a summary of what we just read in the paper. Then we go to work with the weight of the world on our shoulders. We complain:

> *"I don't know why I'm so tired."*
> *"I didn't sleep well last night."*
> *"I just can't get started this morning."*

And we wonder why.

When I suggested to one of my colleagues that he stop watching the news before going to bed and stop reading the paper before work, he replied, "But, how will I know what's going on?"

Most of that information isn't really, "what's going on." It's a biased view of what the media thinks their audience will find interesting and it's shown through a subjective filter that let's very few actual facts through.

And if you're like my colleague who is worried that he won't know what's going on if he misses the morning paper and evening news, stop and think about it for a minute. With the internet and 24 hour live news coverage, "what's going on" is available to you twenty-four hours a day.

So, skip the news and read a book before you go to bed. If you must watch TV, watch a sit-com re-run. If you want to read the paper, save it until you get home from work.

Be selective about the information you allow inside your mind. Stephen Kinzer wrote in *Business Day*, "When people hear nothing but reports of violent crime hour after hour, day after day, they naturally develop a tremendous sense of fear and anxiety. This can lead to a national psychosis that diverts attention and energy away from the many challenges facing the country."

PLUG IN: Find a copy of Norman Vincent Peale's *The Power of Positive Thinking*. Begin reading this book the night before the beginning of your workweek. Make up your mind to read at least twelve minutes right before you go to bed. Do the same thing in the morning during the time you usually spend reading the newspaper. Commit to this program for three weeks and you'll probably finish the book.

If you want to solve the world's problems, begin right where you are. Choose to be the bearer of *good* news. People receive an overwhelming number of negative messages all day long. You can be the one to encourage and energize others.

I KNOW YOU THINK YOU HEARD WHAT I SAID…

…but, what you don't understand is that what I said is not what I meant.

Before I speak, I have something important to say.
– Groucho Marx

In his article, "Now Hear This," Roy Chitwood claims that listening is a sales person's single most important skill. Chitwood divides listening into two types; passive and active. Most people think that listening is simply *not* talking while someone else *is* talking. Actually, there are levels of listening.

Stephen Covey told us in his book, *7 Habits of Highly Effective People*, that there are five levels of listening.

1. Ignoring – making no effort to listen
2. Pretend listening – giving the appearance that you are listening
3. Selective listening – hearing only the parts of the conversation that interest you
4. Attentive listening – paying attention to what the speaker is saying
5. Empathetic listening – interactive listening to understand the speaker's words, intentions and feelings

Empathetic listening, notes Covey, is the most effective level of listening. Because it is interactive, it allows you to see things from your customer's perspective. This, in turn, better prepares you to offer your customer a more personalized solution to his or her needs.

Plug in: When you are busy talking instead of listening, you will often jump in with more information than your customer needs or wants. Soon, you've created confusion by giving the client too much to think about to make a decision. In a sense, you can talk yourself out of a sale.

Listen up! Listen deeply. Listen respectfully. Listen as if what your customer is telling you is a matter of life or death. Actually it is, because your livelihood depends upon it. And if you listen closely, your customer will tell you how you can improve your service.

Leave yourself out of it. Most of us filter what we hear through our own point of view. To keep from doing this, avoid judging what the customer is saying and don't try to second-guess what she's going to say, before she says it. While a key dimension in effective listening is to recognize the speaker's emotional state, don't try to mind read.

Use simple, open-ended questions. Be easy and approachable. Establish a rapport and keep the conversation alive by removing any barriers to effective listening.

THINK OUTSIDE THE BULB

Light tomorrow with today.
– Elizabeth Barrett Browning

IN the electrical wholesale business, we sell thousands of light bulbs. In our industry jargon, we call them "lamps." But, in all of those transactions, not one customer really wanted a lamp. What they wanted was the *light* that the lamp produced. "Light" was the product that they were buying – the *product* of the product; the lamp.

And so it is with every product. A customer doesn't want a lawn mower; he wants a trimmed lawn. A customer doesn't want a car; she wants travel convenience and some want to travel in style. A customer doesn't want a dishwasher; he wants clean dishes.

That's the secret to any sale – to discover the product that your customer is really buying and sell that. Instead of focusing on the features of the product itself, you need to describe the benefits of the features.

"This lawnmower will make your lawn immaculate and it's easy to use."

"The shocks and transmission in this vehicle offer a luxury ride so enjoyable that you'll arrive at your destination refreshed and energetic."

"This dishwasher will sanitize your dishes and is so easy to load the kids will beg you to let them wash the dishes."

Okay, that last one's a bit over the top, but you get the idea. Did we already talk about honesty in our presentations?

 PLUG IN: Sell the product of your product and you will find it much easier and more fun to sell any product. Sometimes you will have to give it some thought.

Not everyone is looking for the same benefits in a product. See each customer differently. Listen for ways that you can make your customer's life easier. Before trying to prove you have a superior product, show the customer ways in which your product will make his or her life better.

IF YOU COULD READ THEIR MINDS

...there is no subsitute for paying attention.
– Diane Sawyer

WALKING into Wal-Mart the first week in January, I nearly tripped over a pallet of Slim Fast. I smiled at this excellent piece of "prophetic marketing" – knowing what the customer wants before she wants it.

Wal-Mart knows that with each New Year nearly every American resolves to lose weight. The diet related products are in place on New Year's Eve.

And Wal-Mart follows this marketing strategy all year long. In February, ice chests will line the high traffic areas within their stores. Patio furniture is on display weeks before spring arrives. School supplies are on the shelves by the end of June. Wal-Mart anticipates each season months before its arrival.

How can you adapt prophetic marketing to your business? What seasons do your customers follow? Are they sports oriented? Do they own a boat? Do they follow the hunting seasons? Answering questions about your customers' seasonal inclinations will offer clues that enable you to anticipate their personal needs.

Another way to anticipate your customer's needs is to be sure you have everything required to use your product. For example, my wife went into a store to buy a mailbox. She picked out one made out of wood. An alert salesman pointed out that she would need to weatherproof the mailbox. He then proceeded to take her to each location for the other products she needed – sealant, sandpaper, brush, paint thinner.

Identifying what your customer wants before she wants it can place you in an invincible position. Any business can furnish customers what they want when they want it, but to give a customer what they want and how they want it before they actually want it, is Customer Service that knows no equal.

PLUG IN: This level of Customer Service is all about strategy. Below are three more ways you can learn to "read your customer's mind."

1. **Help customers to identify their needs.** Some people don't plan for their needs until they become urgent. Convince them of the value of pre-planning. Understand in detail your customer's business to see where your product fits in.

2. **Make it a group effort.** Get together with your colleagues and share information about customers and their product or service requirements. Cooperation is the key to making your business successful. Discuss ideas on problem prevention. Share current

resources of information about each customer.

3. **Explore all of the capabilities** of your products in relation to each customer. You may find that your service or product can help customers in ways they hadn't imagined. Be sure your clients fully understand all of the uses for your product or service.

By using these strategies, you will gain loyal customers, increased sales and less stress from unforeseen problems.

IGNORANCE IS NO EXCUSE

It's what you learn after you know it all that counts.
— John Wooden

On his way to the podium to deliver a commencement address, the dean of a university overheard a student say, "Man, I'm glad that's over with. I hope I never have to open another book as long as I live." The dean said it was the saddest thing he'd ever heard.

Earl Nightingale would tell that story to illustrate the misconception that some people feel their education ends with graduation from high school or college.

You, too, may have thought your education was over after graduation. According to Jean Marie Stine, author of *Double Your Brainpower,* it's just beginning.

Stine says "Without the ability to constantly learn new job skills, throughout your life, you will be left in the dust of the emerging new technologies. The truth is that you will be required to learn up to ten times as much after you graduate as you learned in college just to do and keep your job."

Perhaps at one time you could get by with a formal education; if all you wanted to do was, get by. In today's information age and rapidly changing world, you won't even be able to do that. You may be successful today, but unless you are willing to continue to learn, that is no guarantee you will be successful in the very near future. Just ask Bill McCall.

Death of a Salesman

Bill McCall was one of the top sales reps working for our company. He qualified for our organization's most prestigious award, the President's Club, fifteen years in a row. Then something happened, something that affected the entire world, something big. The "PC" found its way to our desktops. The computer age was born. Gone were the days of hand written sales orders and receipts. No longer was figuring your sales quotas on the back of a ledger pad an accepted practice. The impact the introduction of computers had on the workplace was staggering.

Bill McCall said, "Nothing doing. I've been selling without computers my whole life. I'm not about to change now. I can still sell circles around these kids and their computers."

It is a testimony to Bill's reputation that the sales manager, who had also been around many years before the workplace computer, tolerated this attitude, this refusal to learn something new. Management appointed an assistant for Bill to enter his orders and to keypunch his handwritten budgets into the computer.

It wasn't enough. The change that the computer brought was more dramatic than anyone anticipated. The momentum it generated was unprecedented. Bill McCall could not keep up.

Within a year, his boss brought Bill in "off the street," and assigned him a desk job. Still refusing to learn how to use a computer, he couldn't accomplish much in that position either. A few weeks later, management relocated Bill to a job in the warehouse.

I saw him once during his final days in the warehouse. It was the middle of August and in Texas, it's too hot outside for even the kids to play. There was Bill, probably close to sixty years old, in his white t-shirt, soaked through with sweat. He had a potbelly and the wet shirt outlined heavy rolls of flesh. His hair plastered flat to his head with perspiration, he was one of the saddest human beings I had ever seen.

Within a few weeks, Bill McCall, now a dejected and broken man, left the company. And it was all because he didn't think he needed to learn anymore.

AVOIDING OBSOLESCENCE

When we make the mistake of thinking that our education is complete we cut off opportunities for growth and professional development and in turn opportunities for advancement and greater wealth. The longer we resist continuing education the faster we become obsolete. And if one day we find we are extinct because we no longer know enough to keep up with the pace of our culture, we will find no solace in excuses, because ignorance is no excuse!

PLUG IN: In order to increase your knowledge you will need to enroll in some activities that involve a regular commitment. Saying you will "read more" isn't enough to broaden your base of knowledge. It's a proven fact that we learn the most by being an active participant in the learning process. Pick up a course catalog from a community college or university in your area. Take a continuing education course that you find interesting. Photography, marketing, advanced computer skills, electronic technology, internet and web development classes are a sampling of the variety of courses offered by community colleges. You can learn a second language, swing dancing, team building and fencing. By placing yourself in a learning environment, you also benefit by associating with other learners.

Eric Hoffer said, "In a time of drastic change, it is the learners who inherit the future." According to Price-Waterhouse-Coopers, 70 percent of Fortune 1000 companies cite "lack of trained employees" as the biggest barrier to continued growth. Your commitment to life long learning will assure you a place among leaders who inherit the future and learning will reward you by increasing your value with higher productivity and greater profits.

PHASE 4
Integrity

Be fair and trustworthy, honest and conscientious, and customers will pay you with their loyalty. Act in accordance with these values and you will build a strong and enduring customer base.

Would You Buy From You?

You can never find yourself until you face the truth.
— Pearl Bailey

At the beginning of the twentieth-first century, it seemed that business ethics had become an oxymoron, that integrity was for suckers and that profit was the singular force driving business.

Then, as mega-corporations collapsed and scandalized companies fell, we witnessed the fragile framework of a business built on a foundation without principles. A new focus emerged on old-fashioned values like trust and character. Integrity became important again.

Of course, to the majority of businesses that didn't stray from their values, integrity always was at the core of their company's beliefs. But now, the media is talking about it, seminars are built around teaching it and television dramas weave it into their plots.

It's a fact. Customer Service that excels builds upon a deep-seated trust between client and sales person. Almost any business built to last depends on repeat business and the best way to assure that customers keep coming back is to earn their trust.

PLUG IN: Grade yourself on the following list of questions provided by The Dartnell Corporation.

1. Do you place a high value on having personal integrity?
2. Do you think customers believe you have their personal welfare and well-being at heart?
3. Do you project a straightforward, honest and sincere image?

If you honestly answered, "yes" to all three of the questions above then you probably have a high degree of integrity.

However, all of us are capable of self-deception. If you're really determined to put your honesty to the test, ask three of your friends or family members who know you and your business values, "Would you buy from me?" (Your mom doesn't count – she already thinks you're wonderful.)

Long-term relationships result from long-term trust. The more honest you are with yourself and your customers, the more success you will enjoy.

WHY WOULD I BUY FROM YOU?

A USP is the written equivalent of your essence.
—Raleigh Pinskey

MARKETING leader, Dan Kennedy said it was the perfect example of a *Unique Selling Proposition*. The thirteen words used in the beginning of the pizza chain's rise to success, singled Dominos out from a world of other pizza places.

A USP must answer the question, "Why would I buy from you?" As Kennedy points out, the Dominos' USP does that flawlessly. "Fresh, hot pizza delivered to your door in less than thirty minutes, guaranteed."

Kennedy notes, "It doesn't even say the pizza's good. It simply says that when you order a pizza from Dominos, set your watch, it's on the way." As Dominos moved into larger markets, the company began to phase out the thirty minute or less guarantee.

Once you develop your own USP, it's important to remember from time to time to measure it against changes in the market or a shift in your company's focus. The main thing is to start somewhere. The sooner you can come up with a working USP, the sooner you can begin to focus on what you want to accomplish with your company. The USP will help you to stay on track, to optimize what you do well and to establish a brand identity that separates you from others who are in the same business.

Every business has an individual identity, so it's important to create your own selling proposition that is unique to your organization. Once you develop your statement, it gives you a sense of focus and a rally point for you and your colleagues.

 PLUG IN: Start brainstorming your USP by studying the examples of successful well-known companies.

- *Have you driven a Ford lately?* – Ford
- *When it absolutely, positively as to be there overnight.* – Federal Express
- *Solutions for a small planet* – IBM

By answering the questions below and taking the time to evaluate your results, you can begin to develop the framework for a selling proposition that is uniquely yours.

1. What type of business are you in?
2. Who are your customers and what are their special needs?
3. What unique benefits can you deliver to your customers better than anyone else?

Spend some time thinking about the things you do better than anyone else does. Find a common theme that might connect all of your answers. Word your statement in a precise and compelling manner and you'll be ready to impress the next time someone asks, "Why should I buy from you?"

"ACT ENTHUSIASTIC AND YOU'LL BE ENTHUSIASTIC"

Catch on fire with enthusiasm and people will come for miles to watch you burn. – John Wesley

"**But,** Mom, dying my hair blue will make me '*cool*.'"

This was my fifteen-year-old son's last attempt at giving his mother a logical reason for wanting to change the color of his sandy blonde hair to a bright iridescent blue. His argument hinged on one word – "Cool." That was it. It was supposed to make perfect sense. It was as if he expected his mom to widen her eyes in understanding and say, "Oh, I get it. Sure. Well, honey, I certainly want you to do whatever it takes to be cool."

But, it didn't affect her that way.

It didn't effect me that way either. In fact, his statement triggered one of those "light bulb moments," when a concept long pondered suddenly becomes crystal clear.

I often wondered what happens to the excitement and enthusiasm that almost all of us had as children. The day my son said he needed to be cool, I understood exactly what happened. As you grow up, it becomes un-cool to show enthusiasm. In fact, it's un-cool to show any emotion at all. Even the word itself – *cool* – conjures up an image of something cold and chilly. And that's what we aspire to be when we are young adults – cool.

When I was a new sales manager, I thought my goal was to instill and inspire enthusiasm in sales reps. Over the years, I learned that it helped if an individual already possessed some degree of enthusiasm. Otherwise, "instilling" it was unlikely.

I've seen many skilled and knowledgeable sales people fail because they didn't have any spark or excitement in their presentation to a client. It came across to the customer that they simply didn't care. Many times when I discussed the matter with an individual his response would be, "I'm just not like that. I'm a low-key person. You don't expect me to be something I'm not, do you?"

No, I expect you to be that same little enthusiastic kid you used to be.

Maybe being cool in high school offers some defense to the sarcasm and put-downs that go along with being a teenager. But, for someone in Customer Service, cool is a killer. Customers want to deal with people who are excited about the products and service they sell. They want people with passion and enthusiasm. And since we already learned that saying, "that's just the way I am," is not really an excuse, then how do we get back that enthusiasm and excitement almost all of us displayed as children? Simple. "Act enthusiastic and you'll be enthusiastic!"

———

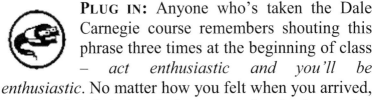**Plug in:** Anyone who's taken the Dale Carnegie course remembers shouting this phrase three times at the beginning of class – *act enthusiastic and you'll be enthusiastic.* No matter how you felt when you arrived, you couldn't help but feel a surge of enthusasm after unifying your voice with 30 others to shout those words.

Carnegie intuitively new what many professional counselors have been telling us for years; *feeling follows action.* In other words, when you feel bored and listless and the last thing you want to do is jump for joy, that is exactly the time you need to jump for joy.

So, when your morning begins with a flat tire, and an overturned garbage can and the neighborhood dogs have dragged your trash all over the street, instead of saying, "It's going to be one of those days," try this instead. Find a secluded place; pump your fist in the air, while shouting three times, as loudly as you can, "Act enthusiastic and you'll be enthusiastic!"

Now, you won't feel or look very "cool" when you do this. In fact, you'll feel and look rather silly, but you *will* feel more enthusiastic. And that, is almost as cool as dying your hair blue in high school.

"Let Me Be Honest With You
…Instead of Lying to You Like I Usually Do"

In a world where people think that the government is corrupt, that the church is corrupt, that the schools are corrupt, show us a business that isn't corrupt and we'll do business with you for life.
– Ryan Mathews quoted in Fast Company – June 2001

WHEN a salesman begins with the words, "Let me be honest with you…" you can't help but wonder what he was being up until then – dishonest with you?

Does that mean you should disregard everything else he said up to that point?

It sounds as if this salesperson is more concerned with *appearing* trustworthy than with *being* honest.

Long-term relationships result from long-term trust. In the beginning of a relationship, you have to furnish evidence of trust. That means you must display trustworthy qualities such as:

- Dependability
- Punctuality
- Accountability

In the beginning, that's all the customer has to go on – the evidence of trust. Consistency supports the evidence over time. Show that you are just as dependable in the small things as you are in the large things and you could earn the loyalty of a customer for life.

PLUG IN: Be consistent in your treatment of all customers. Don't play favorites because of status or money, but give every customer the same amount of respect.

Focus on the following three actions and you will soon earn a reputation as someone who is consistent and trustworthy.

1. **Be accountable.** Take ownership of every interaction with your customer. When things go wrong, take the heat instead of looking for someone to blame. Hold yourself responsible for every outcome.

2. **Follow through.** Make the effort to follow up after the order. Be sure the customer is delighted with the service or product they receive.

3. **Keep promises.** When you commit to your customer that something will happen a certain way, do whatever it takes to make that happen.

By embedding the above actions into your routine, you will give the customer assurance that you are honest and dependable. In a profession filled with mediocrity, you will shine as the standard by which all others are measured.

WATCH YOUR MOUTH!

Your thoughts and words are really units of human energy that either move you towards happiness or away from it.   – Mike Lipkin-Arthur Gillis

EVERY time Scott would make a lousy shot, a stream of profanity surged from his mouth. He reminded me of the expression, *cussin' a blue streak.*

Our foursome consisted of me, two customers, Don and Tommy of Grisham Electric, and Scott. Scott was the vice-president of our company.

At the ninth hole, Scott sliced the ball and sent it blazing off the fairway. Combinations of swear words were strung together in ways that would have made Ozzy blush.

Tommy leaned over to me and said, "Man, your VP sure does swear a lot."

"Yeah. I suppose he does," I said.

Tommy continued, "I guess he doesn't realize that some people don't like it."

I looked at Tommy and understood that he was one of those people who didn't like it.

Our R-rated vocabulary has become widely accepted (tolerated?). Most people don't give the slightest thought, or don't care, that there are still those who find profanity offensive. Tommy is one of those people. He also happens to be a good customer.

He reminded me that clients look for a certain standard of professionalism from their service providers and sales representatives.

And if the fact that there are still customers offended by profanity isn't enough to make you reconsider your word choice, consider the negative impact it has on your attitude.

All of your words are a major influence on your mind set. How do the words, "depressed, lousy, crappy, stupid," make you feel?

How about "excited, pumped, energized, tasty, fresh?"

Words trigger emotion.

They can provoke and they can prevent. Consider these common phrases:

"That's just my luck."

"I never get a break."

"I just can't win."

"I'm not very good at that."

"Whatever can go wrong, will go wrong."

Understand how words can actually shape your day, your week and your life. You probably know hundreds more expressions of some perceived self-inadequacy that you use every day. By repeating statements like these, they become self-fulfilling prophecies. Mentally, you begin to accept these expressions as defining statements of who you are and then incorporate them into your personality. What you say becomes what you get.

PLUG IN: If it were easy to stop swearing, then once profanity lost the charm it held in the schoolyard, it would probably die a natural death as we grew older. Unfortunately, because most of us have been swearing since we were young, it will probably require a lot of effort to stop now.

And of course, all of us have friends who would be quick to say, "But, I don't want to quit." And that's okay, too. However, it's probably a good idea to learn a little self-control, at least in front of your customers. (If you eliminate it altogether, you won't have to worry about "slipping" in front of a customer.)

WHY SWEAR?

First, examine why you use profanity. Is it just lazy language and your response to daily aggravations? Or, is it deeper seated than that? If you find you are always in a bad mood or chronically angry, then swearing isn't helping you to deal with it.

- **Think in clean language**. If you swear a lot aloud, chances are you swear to yourself silently, too. When you find yourself using profanity in your thought processes, ask what alternate words you could use.

- **What if Grandma were here?** On one of those cool spring evenings, when all of the neighbors were sitting in their front yard, my son fell off his bike. Though he wasn't hurt, he shouted the "S" word. As the word echoed through the eardrums of my friends and neighbors, I realized where he'd heard the word. From me. I vowed that day not to cuss in front of my children. Is there someone whose presence prevents you from swearing? Then imagine that person just walked in before you let fly with a string of obscenities. Ask yourself if that's what you would say if Grandma were here.

- **Think positive** Most swear words have negative thoughts attached to them. Verbalize them and you give the negative thoughts more power. Every self-help book ever written, reminds us of what we intuitively know anyway, but can't seem to remember:
Positive thinking produces positive results.
Negative thinking creates negative outcomes.

Pay attention to the words you use. Make it a point to notice and get rid of the negative words that influence your attitude. Learn to use a more empowering language. Become known as someone who "has a way with words." Your positive words will also have an effect on your customers. You can actually make them feel better simply by the words you use to communicate. Remember what Mother Teresa said, "Kind words can be short and easy to speak, but their echoes are endless."

PHASE 5
Initiative

Initiative is the ability to perceive what needs to be done and doing it before someone asks. It is about exceeding the expectations of others.

DID I ASK YOU?

The world belongs to the askers. – Brian Tracy

"I'm going to read aloud the names on your customer account list and then I'm going to ask you some questions about each one. I'll probably be stepping on your toes a little bit. Are you ready?"

"Sure," I said. I was in the office of my manager, Bill Smith. He'd hired me from a competitor, given me an outside sales position and expected immediate results. I'd been with the company three months without much to show for it and Bill was getting a little impatient for me to perform. Hence, the heart to heart talk we were having to shed some light on my lackluster performance.

"Okay," Bill continued. "Here we go. American Industries. How much do you think they spend a month for electrical supplies?"

"Uh. Well… probably about $5000.00."

"You sold them $379.00 last month."

He looked at me and I looked down.

"Okay. Next. Triple A Electric?"

"About $7500.00"

"Mm-hmm. You sold them $489.00. Next we have Barton Construction."

"Well, they're pretty big. They probably buy around $20,000 a month."

"You sold them $1122.00. Congratulations. It seems to be the only account in which you've broken $1000.00."

"Thanks."

"That wasn't a compliment."

"Right. Well, I see your point."

"How about Conroe Inc.?"

"I know what you're driving at." I wanted him to stop!

"Do you? Mike, are you even calling on these people?"

"Yes, sir. Yes, sir. Every week."

"And what do you talk about?"

"Oh, you know. Sales stuff."

"Sales stuff, huh. And do you ever ask them for an order?"

"Well, yeah. Sure, I do. I think so. I mean, don't they know that's why I'm there?"

Bill held up my account list and shook it. "Apparently not!"

He paused to let that sink in, and then he said something that has placed more dollars in my pocket than any other single piece of advice.

"Mike, you have to ask for the order!"

That conversation with Bill Smith took place over twenty years ago, but I've never forgotten it or the impact it made on my sales performance. I know that some of you reading this will be saying, "Well, duh! Any fool knows that!"

But, traveling with other reps, I've seen too many make the same mistake I was making over twenty years ago. And, as I did, they think they *are* asking for the order. But, they're not. Instead, they are saying things like:

"Thanks for the business."

Or

"Well, call us if you need anything,"

Or, even worse,

"You don't need anything today, do you?"

And that's not the same thing as asking for the order.

Only asking is asking.

Asking for the order clearly places in the customer's mind the idea that you are there for business and that your livelihood depends on that business.

―――

 PLUG IN: Practice asking. Go into a convenience store and ask directions. If you really want to be brave and risky, ask for directions to the convenience store you're in. This will help you deal with the fear that people might laugh at you when you ask for something.

Every day make a conscious effort to ask for something that you are unaccustomed to asking for. Ask for help unloading the car, ask for help with a job, ask for help moving. (If you ask that last one too many times, you may lose some friends).

Just ask! Remember, *the world belongs to the askers*!

SERVICE THAT DELIGHTS

"Service that delights is the only thing that counts today- everything else is window dressing."   *– Unknown*

DID you know that having 24 hour room service and a skillful concierge is all you need to call yourself a luxury hotel? Seems like that would be the bare minimum, doesn't it?

According to Price Waterhouse Coopers global hospitality and leisure analyst, Bjorn Hanson, you still get the best service from a bed-and-breakfast. "The owner lives on word of mouth and can't afford an unhappy guest," says Hanson.

It's because B&B owners take initiative to do the little "something extra" that no one asks them to do – the service that delights.

The good news is that anyone can embellish the service of any business simply by taking the initiative to look for ways to surprise the customer. The following stories are examples of just such service and are intended to give you ideas that you might use to create your own Amazing Customer Experience for your clients.

THREE STORIES FROM AUSTIN

Becky Smith got home from the grocery store and unpackaged the chicken she'd bought to prepare for dinner. She decided it wasn't fresh. When Becky called to complain, the store manager delivered to her home a hot roasted chicken from their deli.

When Kenneth Alexander couldn't decide between two lawnmowers, the salesman brought them both to Kenneth's home so he could choose. He then mowed Kenneth's yard with the selected mower.

Most barbers and stylists close on Monday. Curt Fox wasn't sure what to do when he needed a haircut before leaving town to attend a funeral. Curt called Byron's Haircuts where he usually got his haircut. Owner Byron Jenkins always forwarded the phone to his home and when Curt called, Byron opened up his shop and provided the needed cut.

These true stories from an article by Jane Grieg and Dale Rice, found in the Austin American-Statesman newspaper, remind us of what going the extra mile means. And it doesn't have to be as extreme as the preceding examples. Service that delights is often found in the those simple acts of random kindness.

Do Sweat the Small Stuff

One hundred degree temperatures and ninety percent humidity greeted author Mike Lipkin as he stepped off the plane. At the airport auto rental, a car with the air conditioner running and a cold drink in the drink holder awaited him. When Mike asked a manager if it was company policy to place a cold beverage in each car, he smiled and said it was the idea of the young woman who managed the afternoon shift.

A parking attendant picked up a suit and had it pressed and returned to a client's room after the client accidentally called the parking attendant instead of the laundry valet. A pharmacist gave out information about movie schedules when the publisher of the phone book mistakenly listed her number as a movie theater. The manager of the gift shop in a hotel noticed that a client bought M&Ms two days in a row, so she sent a basket full up to his room.

A little thing can make a big difference when you do sweat the small stuff. It personalizes your service. It lets the customer know you do care and makes them feel valued.

PLUG IN: Find something extra that you can do to provide *service that delights.* Buy candy, pay for dinner or provide information when there is no immediate gain for you. By doing this often, you will soon find that the more you give, the more you receive.

Some "Small Stuff" suggestions:
Buy your customer a soft drink
Offer a demonstration
Make a personal delivery
Provide free donuts
Give away a coupon
Email a birthday card or holiday greeting
Send an article about a customer's hobby
Keep candy out for customers

Learn from other businesses that do "sweat the small stuff." Be alert to new ideas. They are all around you. Soon you will discover that the small stuff can make a big difference in your bottom line.

DO YOU WANT TO BE "RIGHT" OR DO YOU WANT TO BE RICH?

Advice is more fun to give than to receive.
– Malcolm Forbes

Is it so important to you to be right, that you correct anyone in error regardless of the circumstances? I'm not talking about moral issues, as in what's right or wrong. I'm referring to the maddening need some people have to be right, no matter what. Even when they're wrong, they're right.

Well, how do you feel when someone tells you you're wrong about something? Even when you know they're right and you're wrong, do you feel grateful when someone corrects you? Do you want to shake the other person's hand and say, "Hey, thanks, for setting me straight?"

I doubt it. Even when you are in error and the person who corrected you is exactly right, you resent the individual who tells you "you're wrong."

Guess what? That's exactly how other people feel when you so magnanimously correct them, too.

———

PLUG IN: Unless something is life threatening, avoid telling anyone they are wrong for an entire week. I know, I know. I hear you saying, "But, shouldn't someone tell them...." Well, maybe someone should and you can bet that someone will. The world is full of people who love to tell other people when they're wrong about something. But, it doesn't have to be you.

THE EXTRA ONE

"If you want to be creative in your company, your career, your life, all it takes is one easy step... the extra one."
–Dale Dauten

MY wife's ninety-four year old mother, Nana, wanted a cappuccino. I'd never heard her order one before. Turns out, she'd been drinking them for some time at Sewell Motor Company of Dallas where she takes her Cadillac for service. Smart thinking on Sewell's part. By the way, this is not the only success story about the legendary car dealer whose motto is, "Obsessed with service since 1911."

(Where do you think Nana likes to take her car for an oil change? The place that's three dollars cheaper or the one that serves her cappuccino? Refer to chapter one about an Amazing Customer Experience.)

Anyway, back to Nana's request. We were on a cruise ship and our server's name was Erika. I believe cruise ships may be one of the last vestiges of truly amazing customer service. For example, Erika's main job was to handle our drink orders and make sure we didn't run out of anything. Erika smiled at Nana's request and quickly disappeared.

Several minutes passed and someone suggested she may have forgotten. No sooner were the words spoken than Erika showed up, flushed and apologizing for making Nana wait.

"The cappuccino machine in our kitchen was broken so I had to go to three other lounges before I found one that had a machine that worked."

Later, we went to the lounge where Erika had gone to get Nana's cappuccino. It was three floors down and on the other end of the ship. Erica literally went the extra mile.

The extra mile is about going beyond the customer's expectations. In order to do that, you first have to know what the customer expects.

How does your industry measure up against customer expectations? Where do you fit in?

PLUG IN: Sit down with pen and paper. Determine the standard that your customers expect from your product or service. That is your benchmark—the measure you need to exceed to go the extra mile.

Brainstorm some ideas for exceeding that benchmark. Write down your ideas no matter how extreme or ridiculous they might seem. Even if you don't do any of the things on your list, you are preparing your mind to be aware of opportunities to go the extra mile.

Soon, it will become second nature for you to recognize the extra mile whenever it appears. Think of it as your contribution to an Amazing Customer Experience. Remember, all it takes is one-step – the extra one.

"If someone forces you to go one mile, go with him two miles."   *– Jesus*

DOES EVERYONE KNOW WHO YOU WORK FOR?

THIS morning, my barber told me how much trouble his brother had in locating a place to buy fifty commercial grade extension cords.

"I could have sold them to him!" I said. "We probably had that many in stock!"

"Really," he stopped trimming my hair. "What do you do?"

"I run an electrical supply house!"

"No kidding? I don't think you ever told me that."

And he was right. I never told him that.

Who knows why we don't tell people where we work and what we do? My guess is that unless we're "doctors or lawyers and such," that we're not especially proud of what we do for a living. So we don't mention our vocation unless someone asks. Then one day someone says, "I was trying to buy a bunch of widgets, the other day…" and we scream, "I sell widgets! I've got the best widgets in town!"

Why not scream it out before someone buys your product or service from your competitor. After all, if you really believe in what you are selling, aren't you doing your friends, family and colleagues a disservice if you let them buy from anyone, but you?

 PLUG IN: Make it a point to tell your barber, your minister, the next person you meet, where you work and what you do. If you're like most people, you're naturally reluctant about blurting out your profession within thirty seconds of meeting someone. You might protest, "But, they might think I'm just trying to sell them something." Which is absolutely not true, because most people are too busy worrying about how they're being perceived by you – and besides, YOU ARE TRYING TO SELL THEM SOMETHING! And they're trying to sell you something, too.

If it's too hard for you to start telling new acquaintances your profession, start by telling the people you already know who don't know what you do for a living. As you get more comfortable, then start telling people your profession when you first meet them. Simply look the individual in the eye, give a firm handshake, tell them who you are and what you do for a living. You never know when someone will say, "Oh, really? You sell widgets? I was just about to buy some widgets!"

DO YOU KNOW
WHO YOU WORK FOR?

YOU are the president of your own company. You're the CEO, the owner and sole proprietor of YOU, Inc. Do you think of yourself that way? You need to.

"But, I'm not. I just work for someone."

Actually, you contract out your services to your employer. You might say they are your biggest client. But, you really work for yourself. If you are unhappy with your employer, then the conditions of your "contract" can be renegotiated or you can contract yourself to someone new.

Each one of us is an entrepreneur. But, most people don't think of themselves that way. Instead, they think like hourly workers, and see their jobs very narrowly defined. When someone asks for something outside that job description, forget about it.

If you suggest that they could improve their lot by giving more to service the customer, they balk at the idea. Actually, keeping the customer satisfied is in their best interest.

When I hear someone say, "Well, they don't pay me enough to do that," I ask, "Would an entrepreneur think like that?"

I am sure that some do – the unsuccessful ones.

PLUG IN: Why not try changing your mindset – your way of thinking – to that of the entrepreneur? Think of yourself as the owner of the company for which you work and apply the same kind of energy you would if you built the company from scratch. What would it hurt to do that for three months?

Perhaps, the company you work for doesn't recognize the worker with an entrepreneurial spirit. After three months, if you feel as though your extra efforts aren't making any difference in the progression of your career, then maybe it's time to make some changes. Do what any entrepreneur would do – cut your losses, regroup and try something new.

Stories have become legends about men and women who left an employer that didn't appreciate their innovative ideas to start their own successful company. They didn't resign to the hourly worker mindset. They followed their independent spirit to new heights of success and opportunity. Follow yours closely for the next three months and see where it leads you.

WHAT CUSTOMER SERVICE CAN'T DO

IT'S a statistically proven fact. More people are likely to tell others their bad experiences with your company than they are to share the good. And the "others" they tell are going to tell their friends, as well.

In retail, we used to say that one unhappy customer would tell ten others, but one happy customer might tell two others. As you can see, an unhappy customer can cause damage exponentially.

So really, even the most amazing Customer Service is simply damage control. You're preventing customers from talking bad about you by minimizing negative word of mouth. But, if you want to produce *positive* word of mouth, it's necessary to go beyond Customer Service.

How do you do that?

Networking.

You may have dismissed networking as a buzzword that referred to a group of mercenaries working a crowded room with a "what's in it for me," attitude. To overcome this image, it might help to examine the root of the word.

Like many buzzwords, this one comes from the computer world. In that industry, the word "networking" refers to a system of computers and databases connected together by communication lines. In business terms, networking is developing a system of people connections through the lines of communication. Obviously, the best way to develop this system is by going to places where people gather.

It's important to remember that this exchange is mutual. You are making available all of your knowledge and resources for the good of the network and others are sharing their knowledge and resources with you.

The ultimate goal is to give and receive referrals. *Almost ninety percent of business is the result of referrals.* By creating your own positive word of mouth networking campaign, you will form new friendships, gain mutual business support and build professional relationships that will last a lifetime.

One of the best ways to start your networking campaign is by joining the Chamber of Commerce. They host networking breakfasts and business after-hours where you will meet prospects and colleagues. Some Chambers offer business lead referrals and business development programs. Get involved with Chamber committees and broaden your networking opportunities even more.

———

PLUG IN: Without a referral, you are just another vendor. Prospects don't know you or why they should do business with you. The following three questions will help you to discover the most effective ways to begin gaining referrals and testimonials.

1. Based on what you know about your prospects, what are the associations that would offer the best contacts for referrals to your target customers?

2. Write a detailed description of your ideal customer. For instance, "My ideal client is in her mid-forties, upper-middle class. She drives a SUV, has a successful career and is on the board of trustees at the local community college." Do you have associates that could refer you to this customer?

3. What existing customers do you have that would give you a referral or a testimonial? Think of how you can make it simple for them to refer you.

Entire books about the power of networking are available at your local bookstore. One of the most comprehensive books about networking I've ever read is Ivan Meisner's, *The World's Best Kept Marketing Secret.*

Since this type of networking is an acquired skill, it would be a good idea to invest in one of these books, so that you can maximize your effectiveness in using this powerful method of growing your business.

PHASE 6
Professionalism

Communicate a consistent, solid image that matches your customer's perception of what is professional for your industry and you create a doorway to success and prosperity.

YOUR ONE-SIZE-FITS-ALL – DOESN'T

Do unto others as they prefer to be done unto.
– Otto Kroeger

"I'LL think about it," said Susanne.

"Is there something you would like me to go over…?" Jerry began.

"No. that's okay," she interrupted. "I just want to think about it."

"Think about what?" Jerry wondered.

Jerry had just finished a flawless presentation of a popular new product. He couldn't comprehend Susanne's hesitation. His close ratio was 90 percent with this product. Her company needs this! Didn't she understand?

What Jerry didn't understand was the customer's refusal to buy had nothing to do with product and everything to do with personality—Susanne's, not Jerry's.

Susanne is one of the four buyer types identified by Mark LeBlanc in his book, *Growing Your Business*. LeBlanc labels the four distinctive personalities as The Thinker, The Doer, The Struggler and the Achiever. Can you guess from those labels, which one is Susanne?

The Four Buyers

A multitude of systems exist that give names to the four personality types and they range back to the time of Hippocrates and his terms of Phlegmatic, Choleric, Sanguine and Melancholy. But for simple and direct application to customer relations, LeBlanc's titles are descriptive, simple and easy to remember.

The obvious reason for learning to identify the four different buyer types is so you can know how to sell to each one. For Jerry to continue to try to *sell* to Susanne would have been useless.

The Thinker

Jerry's best approach would be to *enlist* Susanne in the sales process.

"Susanne, if you were me, what sort of information would you provide to help in making the buying decision." Or, he might simply ask what her time frame is for making the decision, rather than leave it up to her. Thinkers can "think about it," for a long time. By asking for a time limit, he allows Susanne to initiate the follow-up.

Be sure and follow up with the Thinker. If you don't, the next time the buyer wont need to think about it. She will have already made her decision – to buy from someone else.

The Doer

The Doer is ready for action. If Susanne were this buyer type, it would mean she'd decided to buy Jerry's product or service—but, not necessarily from Jerry. With the Doer, you can't waste time. You need to approach them with the same sense of urgency with which they make decisions. Be direct. Get to the point and make the sale. Ask for a purchase order or a delivery date.

THE STRUGGLER

If Susanne's personality were that of The Struggler, she would be prone to over thinking her decision to buy. Too many issues at once flood this buyer's mind. "Is it a good deal? Will it perform? Can I get it cheaper somewhere else?"

Jerry may need to guide this buyer through each issue without being caught up in the struggle himself. If Jerry persuades The Struggler that she's making a good buying decision and then backs that up with a guarantee, he will gain Susanne's trust and become a confidant in future buying decisions.

THE ACHIEVER

Susanne the Achiever sees her purchase as an investment. Jerry needs to convince the Achiever that her company will experience positive results from using his product or service. Susanne the Achiever wants to know the lasting value of making a decision to buy.

The key to recognizing this buyer is that they are planners. They are interested in finding resourceful suppliers who can help them solve their problems. They are more interested in a partnership than a cheap price. Handle this Customer with the attention they deserve and you will have a Customer for life.

As you study and learn these four buyer types, you will eventually be able to identify each one after asking a few questions. Each person has a certain way that he or she likes to be sold. The most successful business people are the ones who don't use a one-size-fits-all approach to selling their Customers.

When you customize your sale presentation to each individual, you will gain a newfound stature in the eyes of those who buy from you and you will gain a feeling of purpose and satisfaction. As Mark LeBlanc states it, "Listen for the other person's mindset, and respond in a way which meets what that person wants and needs. If you do, you will create magic with that person."

PLUG IN: Below is a quick description of each buyer type from Mark's book. Transfer this information to a card that you can refer to when you are planning your sales presentation for a buyer.

---

1. The Thinker is someone who is thinking about buying your products or services – just not necessarily from you.
2. The Doer is someone who has made the decision to buy your products and services.
3. The Struggler is someone who is focused on the costs of buying your products and services.
4. The Achiever is someone who is focused on the outcomes or what happens when they use your products or services.
   —*Mark LeBlanc – Growing Your Business!*

FOR FASTER SERVICE, PRESS "1"

People don't want to communicate with an organization or a computer. They want to talk to a real, live, responsive, responsible person who will listen and help them get satisfaction. – Theo Michelson, State Farm Insurance

A ringing phone drives Bob crazy. I've seen him jump across desks to answer one. To him it's an opportunity calling. He knows that opportunity no longer knocks, it calls on the phone. And Bob believes that the sooner you respond to one opportunity, the sooner another one will come your way. As a result, Bob has more customers than anyone else. Get the connection?

At our company, everyone answers the phone. The result is that everyone knows "the Customer." And of course, this allows our customers to know all of our sales people; a distinct advantage over voice mail.

I understand that voice mail for some businesses became a necessity within the past decade, but I laugh when I hear the recorded message say, "For your convenience, we've automated our phone system." Five minutes later, when I'm still pressing buttons, I ask, "How convenient is this?"

Not long ago, I actually heard one of these recorded messages begin with the words, "For faster service, press 1." Does anyone wait to hear the next option?

Of course, one of the drawbacks to having a live voice answer your phone can be a lack of clarity. To make a point about speaking slowly – articulating – when answering the phone, one day we randomly dialed three local businesses and turned on the speaker so everyone could hear the receptionist answer at each company. This is what we *think* we heard.

Business #1: ***Rozzer n Drozie.***
Business #2: ***Tunnel Lobotomy.***
Business #3: ***Naminey Diddle.***

I know, I know – the speaker does distort the voice some, but then again, the point is to *ar-ti-cu-late* when you answer the phone.

Garbled greetings aren't the only flaws in phone etiquette today. With the omnipresence of automated phone systems, it seems that many people have forgotten the basic techniques and manners involved in using this vital business tool. One of the ways to amaze your customers is to be a professional when you're on the phone.

———

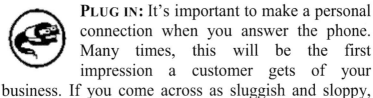

PLUG IN: It's important to make a personal connection when you answer the phone. Many times, this will be the first impression a customer gets of your business. If you come across as sluggish and sloppy, then that is the impression the caller will have about you and your company. Here are some ways to assure that your telephone techniques are professional and up to date.

- **Answer the phone!** Three rings are too many. Smile into the phone. Customers can feel it. Really! Speak clearly and slowly. Develop a system for taking messages and returning calls.

- **Avoid screening calls** – If you feel you must screen calls, then be polite and gracious. When a receptionist tersely demands, "Who's calling?" I want to ask, "Who do I have to be?"

- **Convey a positive image** – Instead of saying, "He hasn't come in yet" or "She left early today," say something like, "He's out of the office at the moment," or "She's out of the office until tomorrow." Use common sense and discretion. Think about how the caller will perceive your words before you speak.

When I'm in a retail store and I hear a phone ringing and ringing, I think of Bob. I can imagine him hurtling counters and leaping over merchandise displays in a single bound to answer it. If you can master just a portion of that reflex that drives Bob to answer a phone at the speed of light, you too, will have more customers than anyone else. And remember, opportunity may only ring once.

YOU'VE GOT MAIL!

Email response time is now considered one of the most important barometers of Customer Service.
— Susan Greco-Inc. Magazine

SOMETHING unexpected happened when the Internet became accessible to most Americans. People started writing again. That was a good thing. It provided people a simple way to stay in touch. It offered more efficient routing of the office memo. And it gave us a new means of communication.

Now entire books are available that tell us how to use this new means of communication effectively. Even the person who hasn't put pen to paper since high school is sending email. Which brings up a case in point. Most companies perform poorly when it comes to email response.

Depending on what type business you're in, email may not yet be a large part of your contact with customers. Then again, it may play a bigger part than you think. You may already be overlooking opportunities to raise the level of your overall Customer Service by neglecting this important tool.

Jonathan Brookner, researching on behalf of consulting group, Peppers and Rogers Group, discovered that 20 percent of the 65 well know internet companies he surveyed didn't respond to email requests at all. On the other hand, 25 percent of the 65 companies responded within two hours. These companies set the standard that the bottom 20 percent will strive to reach in the near future.

Inc. technology columnist Jim Sterne notes that companies who can stay current with email will be the ones to outdistance the competition.

PLUG IN: Why not start today with a commitment to stay current with your email? Even though email may not presently be a key factor in your business, chances are it soon will be. By getting on board now, you can stay ahead of the competition.

One way to manage your email so that you don't spend all day in it is to appoint a certain time of day, to read your messages. For example, read your email at two o'clock every afternoon and respond to all of it at once. That's more efficient than trying to respond to each message as it comes in.

Also, read some articles on email etiquette. In time, this will become increasingly more important and you will be that much further ahead of the herd if you're already versed in a professional manner of using email.

BE A QUICK CHANGE ARTIST

To those who can embrace change and ride it like an industrial surfer, change will be the key to prosperity.
— T. Scott Gross

DON'T you just love change?

Of course you don't. If you're like most people, you dread it. You kick and scream and gnash your teeth when reluctantly forced into the unforeseen future brought about by new technology or innovation. Okay, maybe that's an exaggeration, but not by much.

What's the big deal about change, anyway? Why *do* we resist it so much? What is it that keeps us from bursting with excitement at the idea of something new?

CREATURES OF HABIT

We are comfortable with the familiar. We like routine. We like to use the same coffee cup, go to work the same way and listen to the "oldies" station. Innovation scares us. We hide our fear behind contempt for anything new. We say things like:

> *That's a stupid idea!*
> *What was wrong with the old way?*
> *They just don't make music like they use to.*

Dad always said, "Dance with the one that brought you" and we think that means we must cling to the ways that made us successful in the past. We've forgotten that change brought us to the dance in the first place. Change has always been the signature of our country's ambitious drive to be the starting place of the world's innovations.

According to futurist Edie Weiner, "the cycle of change is heating up for corporations and individuals." Change is going to happen whether we like it or not. We can make up our minds to bring our influence to the change or we can let the change transform us.

———

PLUG IN: Your organization is going to change. It's going to shift, re-shape, transform, mutate, whatever it has to do to remain relevant in the market, or else it's going to die. Listed below are three roles you can play to include yourself in the changes to come, and to influence change itself.

- **Visionary** – *I saw that coming!* You've probably said that before. You anticipated an event prior to its occurrence. For the moment, you were a visionary. Place intention behind the visionary tendencies you already possess. Think back and you will discover there were signs pointing to this moment's latest trend or fashion. Be alert to hot topics in the media, in our culture, in our commerce and you will learn to spot the threads of changes ahead and the shape of things to come.

- **Pacesetter** – Someone has to start the trend. Could that be you? Become known in your industry as the one ahead of her time. The successful business of today and tomorrow will build on change. Your ability to be ready for change before it arrives will place you at the leading edge of your profession.

- **Frontrunner** – Some people and some organizations fail simply because they lack the strength to keep up. Struggling to hold on to the past, they disappear in the dust of innovation and new technology. Those individuals who endure and succeed are the leaders who embrace change without forsaking values.

When you accept change as a way of life, you can thrive on its momentum. In the midst of change, it is important that you remember that there are timeless values providing the foundation that keeps change from evolving into chaos.

Keep your values in place while being flexible. You can't have growth without change. Just think how much further ahead you will be if you continue to grow while everyone else is busy resisting change. The road to prosperity – just like "the extra mile" – is never crowded.

BLAME IT ON THE MICROWAVE

I feel the need...the need for speed!
—"Maverick" – Top Gun

"Ever see a microwave oven before?" Dean asked, motioning me over to the large box sitting on his mom's kitchen cabinet.

The year was 1972 and Dean and I attended the same college. We both needed a break from dorm food and he invited me to his mom's house for a good old-fashioned home-cooked meal – or at least that's what I thought.

We arrived just in time for a lunch that his mother was already busy preparing. I placed my hand on top of this new invention to see if it was hot. Of course, it wasn't.

"I've heard of them. Never seen one before," I replied, examining the box and looking inside the glass on the door.

Dean's mom joined in, "Oh, it's wonderful. I can bake a potato in seven minutes." Right on cue, a loud bell chimed. "There's one now! I can even fix chicken-fried steak in there."

Chicken fried steak is a Texas tradition, a comfort food, and I was fairly certain, even with my limited understanding of how a microwave worked, it couldn't possibly come out right.

Minutes later as I cut into the meat, I knew my assumption to be correct. The crust wasn't – well, crusty – and the meat was chewy. The baked potato was even worse. No matter how much butter I layered inside, it was "dryer than the west Texas sand." My newly formed opinion of microwaves was that they might be fast, but they weren't very good. That was my first lesson about the sacrifices American consumers are willing to make for speed.

Of course, now, thirty years later with the improvements of microwaves and just about every thing else, consumers don't even have to sacrifice for speed anymore. Recently, I caught myself standing in front of a microwave and screaming, "Hurry up! I haven't got all day!"

We live in an age of instant gratification. We have software called *Quicken*, movies titled *Speed* and magazines named *Fast Company*. Our obsession with speed may seem absurd, but one thing is certain; it's here to stay.

PLUG IN: Customers expect to get speed *and* quality *and* price at the entry level. A business has to meet those standards just to qualify for entering the race.

The accelerated pace of our lifestyle means that your customers have even less time to make a decision, to wait for delivery, to hear back from you. Here are three ways you can pick up the pace.

- **Speed up** – Move *faster*. Walk *faster*. Study your business for ways to improve traffic flow.

Arrange your inventory so that your fastest moving products are closest to the point of sale.

- **Act instead of analyzing** – *Execute* is the buzzword for today's Customer Service environment. The very abruptness of the word emphasizes the immediacy of its command – *carry out, achieve, accomplish, finish.*

- **Travel light** – Time to overhaul your processes. Excess paperwork and redundant tasks are no longer acceptable. Look for ways to streamline your operations, such as reducing the number of keystrokes for routine transactions.

Some argue that the obsession with speed is a cause of stress. Some resist the pressure to accelerate their pace. But, whether it's right or not, this time the tortoise will lose.

In the pursuit of amazing Customer Service, the race really does belong to the swift. If you are willing to speed up, to meet the new velocity of business – then you will get to amazing, *faster.*

FIRST IMPRESSIONS LAST

People with little time are more apt to make first impressions as snap judgments, and then base all their later decisions on them. – Harry Beckwith

WHEN you meet someone for the first time, how long does it take you to decide if you like him or her?

Two minutes? One?

How about less than 15 seconds? If you're like most people, you decide immediately. It's the same way when someone is deciding whether to deal with you and the company you represent.

According to psychological studies, ninety percent of people base first impressions on appearance and voice. What is actually said holds almost no influence at all.

Now, how many times has your first impression about someone been all wrong? Several, I'll bet. And often, it's not entirely your fault that you made an error in judgment. It's because the impression the person gives off on first meeting, isn't in alignment with who the person is in actuality. For example, the image they present may seem arrogant and condescending and later you learn that they are shy and self-effacing. Their arrogance is simply a defense and it's inconsistent with who they really are.

In business, you can't afford that inconsistency. Most people aren't going to "wait to get to know you better," before making a judgment about you and your company. So, your first impression needs to reflect that you are trustworthy, confident, friendly and authentic. Then you'd better be able to back up that first impression with genuine values and principles that are consistent with your projected image.

 PLUG IN: Today people are so pressed for time, they form first impressions quickly. Make sure that the first impression you make is in alignment with your values and character. Remove any visual distractions such as a messy work area or unkempt appearance. Refrain from unprofessional habits such as smoking or chewing gum.

Remember that most people make a buying decision based on emotions. If you try to provide Customer Service half-heartedly because your mind is somewhere else, your client will know.

Shake hands, make eye contact and be sure to pronounce correctly the name of your customer or prospect. Be enthusiastic and friendly. *Be amazing.*

Casual Friday is "Out"

A scraggly bearded, young man sat on the curb outside the newly opened restaurant. He was wearing a faded black t-shirt with baggy jean shorts and smoking a cigarette. Bobby and Darlene passed through a cloud of his smoke on their way into the restaurant.

Once inside, they were impressed by the appearance of the servers, all dressed in identical shirts bearing the logo of the restaurant.

The faded black T-shirt guy walked in and started making the rounds at each table. He came to Bobby and Darlene's table.

"Hi, thank you for coming in. Are we taking care of you?"

T-shirt guy was the owner. I don't know why some owners who insist that their staff meet a dress code, think it's okay for them to look like they just came in from mowing the lawn. I suppose the reasoning is, "Hey, I own the place. I can dress any way I want to." That's true. And your Customers can buy wherever they want, too.

But, what if your customers never see you? Vanessa Gardner of Dimensional Marketing provides her Customer Service over the phone. Dimensional Marketing encourages casual dress among their employees and since the company is located near a beach, it isn't unusual for Vanessa's co-workers to show up in T-shirts and flip-flops.

Her first year on the job, Vanessa followed the casual style of her associates, but then had a revelation. "I believe the way you dress makes a difference in how you project yourself and in how professional and confident you feel—even over the phone. My sales doubled my second year, and the third year I was promoted to sales team leader."

Rick Pascal of Pascal and Associates agrees with Vanessa. Rick doesn't believe in casual Friday even though many of his customers have adopted the policy. "Regardless of how they dress, I believe my clients expect me to present the most professional appearance when I call on them. That means a traditional business suit with a tie." Pascal is always mindful of first impressions. "I don't want to walk into someone's office dressed as if I were going to the movies."

———

PLUG IN: First, make sure your clothes physically fit you. Just as important, ask yourself if your clothes fit your image and your business. Are they appropriate for your clientele?

Here is a simple guideline to determine when to "dress for success" or dress down for what's appropriate for your customers.

Mirror the style of your best-dressed clients.

When in doubt, slightly overdress. If you're going to stand out, it's better to stand out as someone who is impeccably groomed than someone who looks like they're on their way to the soccer field.

You can always "dress down" if you arrive at an event and find others dressed more casually. Wear a Polo shirt with a sports jacket to create a business casual look. It never hurts to give the impression that you care about your appearance. Dressing well is an expression of respect to others and helps to project a professional attitude.

PHASE 7
Ownership

Taking ownership of your life and your problems will set you apart from your competitors and from almost everyone else. Customers love the person who can own up to a problem, a mistake, or a challenge and turn it into a triumph.

WE MAY DOZE,
BUT WE NEVER CLOSE

If you want your dreams to come true, don't sleep.
—Yiddish Proverb

Sleep is overrated. – Bobby Casilhas

IT was ninety degrees at 7:00 that morning.

When the air conditioner at our business broke down at 4:00 in the afternoon, it was 105 degrees outside. Within minutes the inside temperature rose ten degrees. I called the A/C repair service.

"First thing in the morning," she promised.

"Well, okay, if that's the best you can do."

"It's a busy time of year!"

"I know. Oh, can you send Keith. He usually works on it, so he's familiar…"

"Well, if he's got time," she interrupted. "He's got other jobs before yours."

Keith showed up at 5:05 that same afternoon. I stared at him in disbelief. "They said it would be tomorrow."

"Got another job in the morning. Thought maybe I could fix you up this afternoon. If that's alright with you."

Yes, it was all right with me. He had our air conditioner working by six o'clock that evening.

When Keith left his employer a few months later to go to work for another company, our business went with him. Five years later when Keith started his own company, we followed him again.

The first week he was in business for himself, he got a call from a commercial customer who'd lost air conditioning at 3 AM. Keith had their system running again before daylight. The "24-hour service" on his business card is no idle promise.

Keith Deaver could have viewed himself as just another hourly worker. But, instead, he viewed each job as an opportunity, a chance to provide service beyond a customer's expectations. He didn't look at his work from a "what's in it for me," point of view. He took service to the next level. And it paid off for him.

It paid off for Keith because clients forgot the name of the company that he worked for and only remembered his name. So when Keith Deaver went into business for himself, his customers followed.

———

 PLUG IN: For ninety days, imagine that you are the owner of the company that employs you. What would you do differently that you're not doing now?

Provide the service that you would if the entire business depended upon you. Make it convenient for your customers to reach you around the clock. Use an after-hours answering service or an automated voice mail with a paging capability so that your customers are only a phone call away.

Shut Up
and Have a Nice Day!

Any fool can criticize, condemn and complain and most fools do. – Dale Carnegie

"Well, we're short handed today. We've got two people out on vacation and another called in sick."

Jim was explaining to purchasing agent Pete Manning, why an order was late. But instead of sympathizing, Manning shouted, "I don't care about your internal problems! All I want is my order when it was promised!"

Usually customers don't react as strongly as Pete Manning did. In fact, most customers will tell you they understand. But, they make a mental note not to depend on you or your company in a crisis. Then there are other customers who won't say anything at all. They simply won't call again.

When your company has lay-offs, budget cuts or policy changes that affect service, refrain from telling your customers about it. When you're having a bad day, a fight with your spouse, or you're just plain stressed out, keep it to yourself.

Resist the urge to use your problems as excuses for poor performance. Your customers and associates may sound sympathetic but they are probably already looking for someone else who doesn't buckle under pressure. As the saying goes, when you tell people your problems, half of them don't care and the other half are glad you have them.

And who can blame them? After all, they want you to solve their problems, not add your problems to their own. Customers want to be able to depend on you to deliver your product or service. They want to place their faith in you that you will make everything turn out all right.

Most customers have been lied to so many times that when they do find someone who keeps commitments without whining, they will gladly pay with their loyalty and cash.

 PLUG IN: Like it or not, you have to provide your customers with the emotional security that you may not be getting yourself. You're a motivator, a friend, the confidante who understands the challenges your customer faces. You are the stress alleviator, the problem solver, and you "keep your head, when all those around are losing theirs." You're the one who promises "Everything will be alright," when circumstances say otherwise.

You are the one to *make it happen*. Put on the smile, act enthusiastic; take the action necessary to keep the promise. Customers are cynical because they've been promised so much and received so little. Be the one to restore their faith. Work the extra hour. Make the extra phone call. Walk one more mile. Never let the customer know your complaints. Just shut up and have a nice day!

LIGHTEN UP!

If you're not having fun, you're not doing it right.
−Unknown

"THIS is my Mocha Cocoanut *Frappa-Cappa-cino* Dance!" said the young woman behind the Starbucks counter. She began sliding and shimmying while a familiar disco song played in the background. As I looked around, I noticed all of the customers laughed and applauded their approval. The other staff behind the counter watched her dance and joined in when they picked up her moves.

Starbucks calls the people they hire, "partners" and the servers behind the counter are *baristas*. Barista is an Italian word that translates roughly as "one trained to make and serve coffee." I've read that in Italy it is a coveted title.

While the Baristas were dancing, they were shouting out drink orders. Hot beverages were passing across the counter and money was changing hands. Every one was too busy having fun to notice that business carried on as usual.

The Baristas at Starbucks make it look as if it's fun to work there. The customers pick up the energy the Baristas generate and soon they are having fun, too.

When someone says to me, "I don't understand how people will pay five dollars for a cup of coffee," I tell them it's not about the coffee; it's because it's fun to go to Starbucks. And that is no accident – it's by design.

Part of providing an Amazing Customer Experience is to give your customers, and your colleagues, permission to have fun. Research indicates that the most productive employees work for businesses that encourage them to enjoy their job and that enlist the customers in on the fun, as well. Studies show that when people have a choice of where to buy the same service or product, *90 percent* will go to the place that they consider the most fun.

PLUG IN: Get together with two or three co-workers and ask this question of yourself, your colleagues, and your boss. "What can we do to make our work environment more fun for employees and our customers?" Study the places in your community where people go to have fun. See what you can duplicate, borrow or adapt from their business to yours.

Get back together and brainstorm. Be open-minded and let your creativity flow. Make an agreement not to laugh at each others' ideas. Share from your experiences and record your ideas no matter how absurd they may seem. Once you exhaust your efforts, look back over your list. If you've been open and creative, you will discover at least three legitimate ideas you can use to Lighten Up your workplace!

SEE YOURSELF SUCCEEDING

You have to be very careful if you don't know where you're going, because you might get there.
– *Yogi Berra*

"SEE Yourself Succeeding" is a trademarked phrase used by Fidelity Investments. What a great outlook! To "see yourself succeeding," you must first believe that you can be successful. Once you've mastered that, the next step is "seeing" or envisioning your idea of success. In other words, when you are successful, what will that look like? Where and how will you live? Will a certain amount of money define success? What is your lifestyle like in your vision of success?

Is it important that you visualize your success? **It's vital.**

Visualize down to the last detail – the color of your home, the type of car you drive, the clothes you wear. And remember, you will never enjoy a satisfying success that just focuses on material things. You must also visualize the condition of your family life, your spiritual life and your friendships.

Perhaps you're one of those who think visualization is hokey and smacks of new age mumbo jumbo. Then examine the lives of those who've successfully used it for centuries, from the Olympians of ancient Athens to the modern professional sports icon – the athletes.

TIGER, CELINE AND RUSSELL

REPORTER: "If you win this tournament today, you will become golf's first ten million dollar man. Did you ever think you would *see* that?
TIGER WOODS: "Yes."

A few hours after that interview, Tiger Woods became golf's first ten million dollar man.

Celebrities, too, are familiar with the importance of a strong, clear vision. Celine Dion said she imagined her diva like success since she was five. Russell Crowe said during his Oscar acceptance speech, "This is the fulfillment of a boyhood dream."

 PLUG IN: See yourself succeeding. Imagine positive outcomes. Know what you want. Focus on what you want to do or be more than on what you want to have.

1. Visualize the results you want to produce at the end of your day, your week, your year.

2. Write your vision down in explicit detail on a card that you can carry with you.

3. Read it within twenty minutes of awakening in the morning and twenty minutes before you go to sleep at night.

MR. POTATO HEAD, UNPLUGGED

Funny is an attitude. – Flip Wilson

"So, now that you're the manager, what are you going to do first?"

When I was a salesman, I would often announce, "If I ran this place, the first thing I would do is _____!" Fill in the blank– raise commission, fire everyone and start over, double the inventory – whatever fit my rant of the week. Then one day, I got the chance. I received the promotion to manager of the store where I served as an outside salesman for fifteen years. Time to live up to the big talk.

"So, what's the first thing you're going to do?"

"The first thing I'm going to do is buy a Mr. Potato Head," I replied.

"What? Why!" asked my colleague.

"I'm going to set him on the counter. It'll give the electricians something to do while they wait for their order."

"You mean electricians like Bubba, who weighs two-fifty, enjoys bar room brawls on the week-end and gripes the whole time he's at the counter? You think guys like him are going to play with Mr. Potato Head?"

"Yes, I do," I assured him. I really had no idea.

Later that day, Bubba walked in.

"What the heck's this?" he demanded, picking up the defenseless toy. Then he answered his own question, "Dang Potato Head." He chuckled, "Hadn't seen one of these since I was a kid."

The next thing we knew, Bubba was giving Mr. Potato Head an extreme makeover.

Bubba proved there's still a little boy inside the toughest exterior. Mr. Potato Head was the first of many additions to our counter. It became apparent that the best way to ease the customer's wait is to give him something to do while waiting.

In this age of microwave ovens and instant coffee, customers have little patience when it comes to waiting. However, research indicates that most people don't mind waiting, *if* they perceive the wait as part of the experience. Get your customers *doing* something as soon as they enter your business. Provide them with ways to occupy the time while waiting and the wait will seem minimal.

———

PLUG IN: If you have a waiting area or a sales counter in your business, place classic "unplugged" toys for your customers to play with like, Mr. Potato Head and Etch-a-Sketch. Tavern puzzles and Rubik's cubes are also challenging and time consuming. If you don't think your customers will play with toys like these, then hide and watch. Just like Bubba, you'll discover that inside each one of us is a five-year-old who loves to come out and play.

Are Your Customers Invisible?

I'll never forget being ignored by the two "greeters" hovering over the seating chart in the restaurant lobby. My high school sweetheart, Tandy Holter, and I stood a few feet away and waited. The two greeters never acknowledged us. They continued their discussion as if we weren't there.

After standing for a few minutes in awkward silence, Tandy giggled, turned to me and asked, "Are we invisible?"

It was funny to a couple of sixteen-year-olds and it broke the tension. One of the women looked up and snapped, "How many?"

Though it happened over thirty years ago, I still remember that moment. It's a powerful illustration of just how long we remember bad service. Forever.

It was our first impression of the restaurant. It was our last impression. We never went back.

The Joke is On …

In a similar incident, Bob told me about waiting at a counter while the parts guy read the paper. He said he noticed a little cartoon-like statuette of three comical characters, stooped over clutching their stomachs and roaring with laughter. The caption engraved across the base of the sculpture reads, "You Want it When?"

Bob remarked, "Did you ever notice that the places that have those little jokes about service are always the places where the service *is* a joke?"

Well said.

At the other end of the Customer Service spectrum is locally owned, Take 1 Video. When you walk in the door, there may be a counter full of people waiting in line to rent videos and games. It doesn't matter. You will hear a greeting as soon as you cross the threshold. In fact, if you've been there more than twice, they'll call you by name.

If you ask about a certain movie, a Take 1 staff member will walk you over to its location, pick up the product and place it in your hands.

The point is, "being busy," is no excuse for not acknowledging a customer the minute they enter your business.

PLUG IN: Simple. Stop what you're doing – discussing the seating chart, reading the paper, gossiping about your boss – and say, "Hello!"

Greet customers as soon as you see them, and make it a point to see them as soon as they walk in the door. If customers drop by your office unannounced don't send your receptionist out with a terse, "You have to make an appointment."

Your customers don't *have* to do anything. If your best friend you hadn't seen since high school walked in, you wouldn't say, "Call back later, make an appointment, or take a number." You would see them right then.

Even if you're busy. It's that important.

A SATISFIED CUSTOMER NEVER IS

In the new millennium, customer engagement is where it's at. – Smith & Rutigliano; Discover Your Sales Strengths

FACE it. Satisfaction is the bare minimum, the baseline, for customer retention, but it is no guarantee of your customer's business tomorrow. Think about it this way; a customer can be satisfied with your company and your competitor at the same time.

Customer satisfaction simply isn't enough to keep your clients from switching to a competitor when they perceive a better offer. Note that "better offer" doesn't always mean a cheaper price. In fact, though price may sometimes drive a customer to make the initial purchase from a business, it has almost no effect on retaining that same customer.

So, what keeps customers coming back? According to Gallup surveys, *customer loyalty* is the main component that drives repeat purchases. And what's the biggest factor in building customer loyalty?

You are.

Gallup found that customers who felt "strongly positive" about the people they bought from were twelve times more likely to continue to buy. In other words, the people play a bigger part than the product in keeping customers coming back for more.

PLUG IN: How do you instill customer loyalty? You "engage" the customer. Engage is a buzzword that means to involve your customer emotionally with your business.

Okay. So, how do you do that? In the same way you would build loyalty in a friend. You develop a strong relationship based on confidence and integrity. Below are the four dimensions of customer engagement from the book, *Discover Your Sales Strengths*.

1. **Confidence** – Customers feel that you are trustworthy and that you keep your promises.

2. **Integrity** – Customers feel that you treat them fairly.

3. **Pride** – Customers feel good about your product or service and feel that using your product reflects well on them.

4. **Passion** – A strong relationship exists between the customer and your business when the customer sees you as irreplaceable.

You already have these qualities to some degree. The more you can engage these traits within your personality, the more you will engage your customer's loyalty.

"Do You Speaka My Language?"

"**O**KAY, I'll IBT those A1410's from DCH. UPSR will be the best way to get them here."

Huh? That's an actual statement I overheard one of our salesmen make to a customer over the counter. I saw the look of confusion on the customer's face.

"Does that mean my material will be here tomorrow?" he asked.

"UPSR. Nooner. For sure."

I stepped up to the counter to offer my services as a translator.

"Yes, sir. He's going to have your material shipped in by UPS overnight service. It will be here tomorrow by noon."

"Oh, thanks. Why didn't he just say that?"

Now the employee looked confused. "I thought I did!"

Your industry has its own jargon full of acronyms, abbreviations and other gobbledygook that you've used so long it has become part of your language. But, it's probably not the same as the language your customer speaks.

Unless it's important for your customers to understand the jargon of your industry, don't bother trying to explain it to them. Just translate it into non-jargon terminology and give it to them straight.

For example, in our company we use the acronym IBT for Inter-Branch Transfer. Even telling the customer what the letters stand for, is still borderline jargon. So, the best way to describe an "IBT" is to say, "We'll ship your product in from one of our other locations."

 PLUG IN: Be aware of your industry specific jargon. You may not even recognize all of it, because it's become second nature to you. Sometimes you need to go to a friend outside of your business and ask if they know what a specific term or phrase means.

The following are three ways you can reduce the amount of jargon you use with a client.

- Learn to identify the acronyms and jargon that are specific to your business.

- Be able to translate your jargon into plain English. Never assume your customer understands your language.

- Educate your customer to your jargon only if it will make it easier for her to do business with you.

WANT FRIES WITH THAT?

"**Y**OU ruined my vacation!"

"But, you were in such a hurry..." the flustered sales clerk tried to diffuse his customer's anger.

"I trusted you," the customer continued. "You were supposed to take care of me. I told you to sell me whatever I needed to go with the video camera I bought from you. I took my family to Disney World and in less than an hour, the battery ran down. Why didn't you sell me an extra battery?"

Harv Eker shares that story from his experience as an electronics salesman in *The Aladdin Factor*, by Jack Canfield and Mark Victor Hansen. Harv said he felt "like death warmed over" and learned never to assume he already knew what a customer wanted without asking the customer first.

You can't drive through a fast food restaurant without the offering of "upsizing, combos or value packs." The phrase, "want fries with that" has become part of our vernacular. It's simply a method of increasing sales called "selling-up."

Some people dismiss this as another expression of corporate greed. I disagree. Harv's story is a case in point.

I've been in convenience stores to buy milk and been reminded that, in fact, I do need bread. I have bought batteries with the flashlight, new film when I picked up developed photos and an extra ink cartridge with a new printer all because of salespeople who made the suggestions. Later, I was grateful to each of these representatives of amazing Customer Service when I had fresh batteries during a power outage, extra film for the camera when my grandson smiled, and a refill for a printer that ran out of ink at midnight.

In each of these cases, the extra money I spent at the time of my initial purchase was well worth the anxiety that it saved me later. When you make the effort to sell your customer the accessories that go along with the product, it's a mutual benefit.

A colleague of mine expressed another benefit of "selling-up" recently. He told me that he calculated that if his sales for accessories had increased just three percent, he wouldn't have had to lay people off during a business slump. By asking the customer for the extra order, people could have saved their own jobs.

Though you will get an occasional grump who barks, "If I wanted something else, I'd ask for it," most people are appreciative of the extra effort you take to "sell-up."

MAKE IT FUN

In an organized effort to sell-up, our company ran a promotion on lamps. A banner hanging behind our counter area said, "We'll give you a dollar if we don't ask you about lamps with your order." Over the sign were dollars bills hanging from a clothesline. It engaged the customer's interest. Because we see the same customers almost every day, it turned into a game. The customers would pay close attention to our salesmen, hoping they would forget to ask. And it kept us more alert to selling, rather than just taking orders.

PLUG IN: You might interest your boss in paying an extra incentive for reaching a quota of accessory items. Or, if you are the boss, consider a program that gives your sales people incentive to sell more. Here's a three-step plan for increasing sales by selling up.

1. **Choose a product**. Write down the product name, then write below it all of the possible accessories that you could sell with it.

2. **Practice how you ask.** Role-play with co-workers until you are comfortable with your dialogue.

3. **Choose your words wisely.** Sell-up from a positive point of view. Ask, "How about some ice cream to go on top of that pie?" rather than "You don't want ice cream on that, do you?" Instead of "Will that be all?" say, "What else do you need today?"

In the new economy, it pays to sell up. You are providing an extra service to your customer and an added source of revenue to your company. Selling up creates a professional image that identifies you as a specialist in your industry.

The Most Important One

My father says that almost the whole world is asleep. Everybody you know. Everybody you see. Everybody you talk to. He says that only a few people are awake and they live in a state of constant total amazement.
–Patricia Graynamore

Since you've read this far, my guess is that you are one of the few who *are* awake. You live in a state of constant total amazement.

Stay alert and pay attention to the opportunities that fall at your feet every day.

Keep learning and discern the knowledge that leads to wisdom.

Be mindful of laughter and understand the value of mixing humor with enterprise.

Remember that the most important factor in the success of any endeavor in which you are involved, is you.

In fact, it takes *u* to spell s*u*ccess.

"… I kept back nothing that was profitable unto you"
–Acts 20:20

FINAL THOUGHT
"IT TAKES SO LITTLE TO BE ABOVE AVERAGE"
—Florence Littauer

There is scarcely anything in the world that someone cannot make a little worse, and sell a little more cheaply. The person who buys on price alone is this man's lawful prey.
– John Ruskin

"**W**HY should I buy from you anyway?"

That question still rings in my ears though I heard it over twenty years ago in the office of Dave Gifford, the purchasing agent for a company that was easily our biggest client. The reason for my visit was to apologize for a shipping error we had made. Our mistake had cost Gifford's company expensive down time. All my apology had done was prompted his question, *"Why should I buy from you anyway?"*

Our company needed Dave's business. *I* needed Dave's business. And Dave needed a reason why he should continue to give it to us.

Shuffling my feet and managing a goofy grin didn't bring a hint of a smile from Gifford. The only thing I could think of to say was also the dumbest thing I could have possibly said, given the circumstances of my visit. I finally managed to stammer out, "Uh, because we have...uh, better service?"

"B-E-E-E-P!" He imitated the loud buzzer that sounds on a game show when a player gives an incorrect answer.

"Wrong!" Then he *did* smile, as he said, "Your service is just as bad as everyone else in town. The only thing you have that your competitors don't, *is a salesman who calls on customers to apologize for how bad the service is!"*

I shrank as Dave Gifford said those words. He was telling me that my company wasn't extraordinary. It was just average.

Someone said that the average American thinks he isn't. That seems to hold true of the average business as well. Of course, no business would dare label itself as "average." After all, would you want to eat at a place claiming to be an "average restaurant"? How about letting someone work on your automobile who advertises as "your average local mechanic"? When you need an attorney, are you going scan the phone book looking for an "average law firm"?

Yet most businesses are exactly that – average. And they don't even know it. They think their product or their service is better than it really is. In a time when mass customization has raised customer expectations about service to a level higher than it's ever been, in many businesses Customer Service has dropped to an all time low.

However, most companies are unaware. Instead, they think their Customer Service is better than it's ever been, thank you very much. They believe that the innovations brought on by technology have improved the level of Customer Service. And they want the customer to believe that, too.

But, technology alone isn't enough to raise the level of Customer Service. And, technology isn't the problem. It's not even an issue. What is an issue is our love affair with complacency brought on by our dependence on technology. We no longer have to add numbers in our head, answer our phone, or count change. Automation does all of that for us. We've become so comfortable in our lifestyle that we see anything that requires effort as an evil. So, we focus on eliminating the evil – discomfort – at the price of performance.

To perform requires effort and effort often implies discomfort. Leaving our comfort zone takes on new meaning.

It is my sincere hope that the ideas in this book will inspire you to leave your comfort zone and explore the deeper meaning behind service.

In your own mind, you know what you need to do to excel. Do that.

In your heart, you know what you need to be to soar above the average. Be that.

Once you leave your comfort zone, once you raise the bar on performance you can never lower it again. You can't go back.

Why would you want to?

To perform at a consistently higher level than others – that's the mark of a true professional.

-Joe Paterno

About the Author

Mike Dandridge is a corporate trainer and sales manager for Rexel, Inc. This book is the result of 30 years of experience and research in wholesale and retail sales management.

Mike is a captivating professional speaker and an engaging educator. He speaks on the application of faith-based principles to achieve optimum results in performance, productivity and personal development. Mike personalizes his programs for individuals and groups seeking extraordinary business success and personal fulfillment.

Mike is also author of ***The Divine Spark, Seven Golden Keys to an Extraordinary Life,*** and a professional member of the National Speakers Association.

He lives with his wife, Francesca, in central Texas.

Mike encourages you to contact him via email with feedback or to share your ideas about how to amaze customers.

Bring Mike to your next meeting or convention and give your group an Amazing Customer Experience.
Call 254-773-5357 to discuss your event and request a speaker's kit.

mike@highvoltageperformance.com
www.highvoltageperformance.com

Order Form

You may order more copies of *Thinking Outside the Bulb,* by sending in the completed form below with payment via check, VISA, or MasterCard or you may order online at www.highvoltageperformance.com

---

Payable in US funds only.
Mail your orders to:

High Voltage Performance   Bill my credit card #:
P.O. Box 3601   _____
Temple, TX   Exp. Date: _____
76505   [ ] MC [ ] Visa

Signature: _____

Ship to: _____

Address: _____

City: _____ ST _____ ZIP _____

Paperback books: $17.00 x _____ **# of copies =** _____

Hardbound books: $23.77 x _____ **# of copies =** _____

                Subtotal: _____

Postage $3.00 per book: _____

Total amount due: _____

This offer is subject to change without notice. Please allow 2-3 weeks for delivery.